MOM...IT'S CANCER

They all said she was much too young.
They were all very wrong.

JULY 30, 2020

DEBBIE LEGAULT

1

First Printing July 2020

https://momitscancer.godaddysites.com/

Oh the places you've gone and the people you've met
Many changes in time as you've grown, yes, and yet
Still each sister. when the the load gets too much on the back
Knows there's two in her corner to take up the slack

As your parents we feel such a great sense of pride
That it's hard to keep all of the proudness inside
As we rock on the porch of the end of our time
We will hold hands and know that what we leave behind
Is the power of sisters times one, two and three

Our girls Adrienne, Isabelle and Stephanie

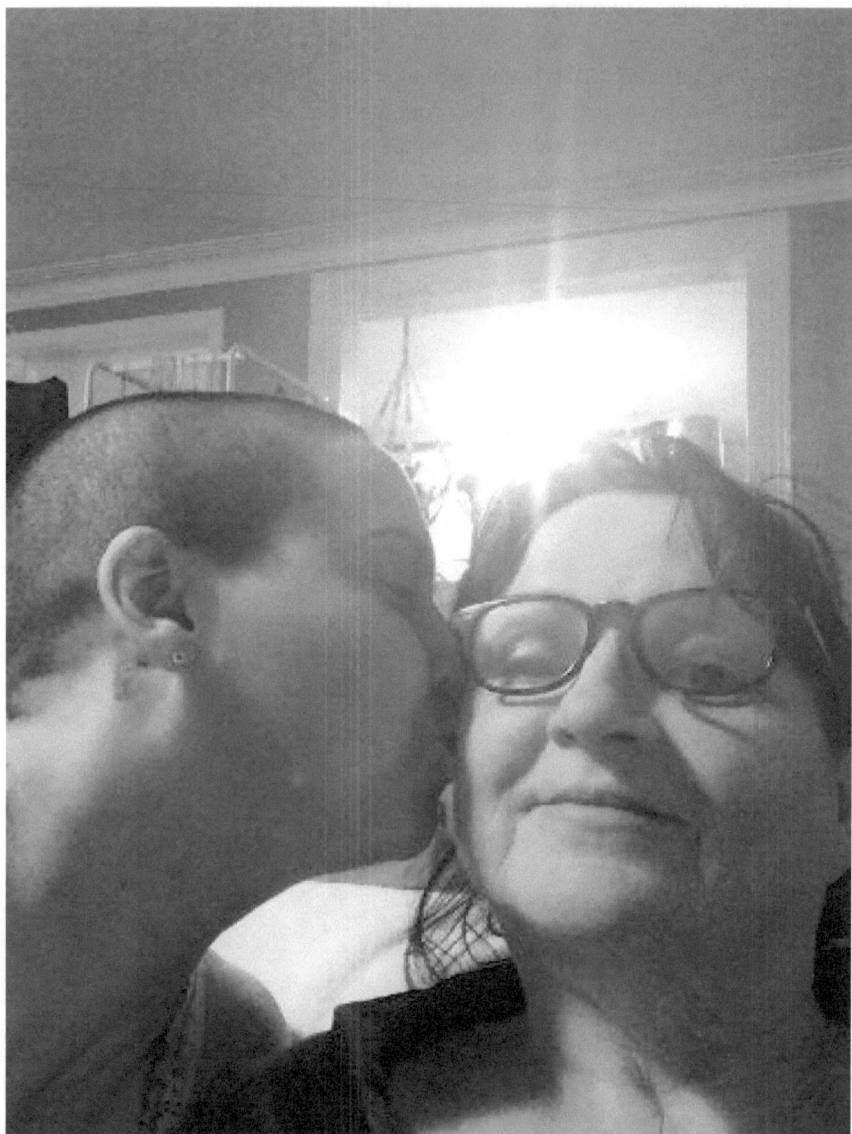

Prologue

I have lived a fairly blessed life. I was lucky enough to find a life partner who gets me, who has grown with me over the last 34 years as we have lived our very unusual life and raised our three children together.

Adrienne is our middle child. Her older sister Stephanie was very good working materials when it came to parenting. She reasoned through things at a young age and made it very easy for me to gain her trust when it came to things like wearing a coat because it was cold outside or resisting peer pressure when it came to bullying or drinking. Her younger sister Isabelle is an observer, who made the vast majority of her behavioral decisions on what kind of consequences she saw came from breaking the rules. She's a sleeper child, the kind who surprises you by coming at you with valid arguments when she needs a rule to be bent or her horizons broadened because she has learned what works.

Adrienne is the type of child who learns everything by experience. As an example, I learned she could swim when she jumped off the end of the dock into the river just as I turned my back to put down the towels when we were visiting her Grandmaman…when she was three. In .0008 seconds, I had to understand that I could not transfer my fear to her because she was, indeed, keeping herself above the water. I encouraged her to keep doing it right back to me at the edge of the dock. I pulled her out, told her how impressed I was that she had done so well, and made a deal with her that she would not do that again when I wasn't looking. Not because she couldn't swim, but because I needed to be watching her. Oscar worthy acting skills on my part, since my heart was pounding in my chest and all I wanted to do was squeeze the life out of her with relief that she was okay. But I couldn't tell her she couldn't swim, now could I. Because she had just proved to me that she could.

Needless to say, she was quite a shock to the system after Stephanie, especially because there are four years between them and my success with Stephanie made me pretty confident that what I was doing worked. And it did. With Stephanie. Not so much with her little sister.

From what I have heard from my older siblings, Adrienne is me as a child. It is a great gift, being given the opportunity to raise yourself. It gives you a toolbox to rummage through when you're trying to figure out what to do, in many cases because you know exactly what NOT to do, what didn't work with you, what made you feel very small, what wounded you the most. As you raise a child like Adrienne, you are given the amazing treasure of healing your own wounds, of realizing forgiveness for days past, because you become aware of how deep you have to dig to find the right words or actions, how exhausting it can be, and you know that your life circumstances have given you the luxury of having that kind of time and energy.

All my children all magical beings to me, each with their own strengths, each with their own limitations that they try very hard to acknowledge and work within. But Adrienne always had to fight a little bit harder, to go against some of her own instincts because she knew that following that path would not bring her to a good place. She had to get up every day and not give up, not take the easy road, tell herself that she could do it. She had to acknowledge the limitation of learning everything by experience and trust that in some cases, she had to do what the rules said because the outcome would be of benefit. When I look at her, how much she has accomplished, I am filled with pride, both in her and myself. Adrienne is, simply put, my masterpiece.

In the last few years, Adrienne's life has settled. She has a job she loves that feeds her mind and her spirit. She is living in a city in which she feels a strong sense of rightness, of belonging. She has wonderful friends, who share her zest for life and love for spontaneity. It gave me such comfort, such joy, to think that most of the battles were behind her, that all the incredibly hard work she had done to get her where she is was finally paying off. That I could put down my paintbrush, that with the occasional touchup my masterpiece would continue to stand as a testament to the trust that she had that I would never lead her astray, that my belief in her was justified, that she could trust her own decisions. She could look at her own life and know that she could believe in herself.

Silly me, thinking that the universe was done with her.

Adrienne began investigating a lump she found in the shower in February 2019. She had to push, sometimes a little, sometimes a lot, for the medical professionals to take her concerns seriously. First an exam, then an ultrasound, then a biopsy. Then on March 15th, 2019 I got a phone call that would change my life forever.

"Mom…it's cancer."

My 27-year-old daughter, my masterpiece, whose life was on such a good path, had just been told by her doctor that she had breast cancer. The shock of it was so intense that typing those words over a year later still brings on a physical reaction. There is no family history. There were no risk factors. She is a typical young woman of her age, following the mantra of everything in moderation. There is nothing to look at to cast blame, to find a reason. The universe spun the wheel of chance and it stopped on my 27-year-old daughter getting cancer.

I knew that day that I would be there with her for whatever came after. That is the type of mother I am, and my life situation allowed for me to do that without the rest of my world blowing up. I packed up my life and moved into her one-bedroom apartment, sleeping in the living room for almost a year.

One thing that became clear along the way was how much of an outlier Adrienne is. There are a lot of support services out there for parents of young children and teenagers who have cancer. There are a lot of support services for older women and their families going through breast cancer treatment. There is almost nothing out there for women like Adrienne who are diagnosed in their twenties or early thirties. They share parts of their cancer stories with the others, but there are so many aspects of dealing with breast cancer at her age that make it different. And as her caregiver, as the person doing all I could to minimize the trauma, the pain, the loss, there was almost nothing out there for me, either.

I am the rock, the center of my family's universe. I always have been. But this experience tested me to the limits and beyond. To help me along the way, many people suggested that I journal about it as a place to express my thoughts and feelings. This book is a compilation of the pages I wrote to help me cope with what is to date the most devastating time of my life. I am sharing this experience with the world in the hope that other mothers like me, with daughters the age mine was at when she was diagnosed, can find common ground, can prepare themselves for what they will go through watching their children fight the battle of their lives. That they will have a few more tools to rummage through when the walls are closing in.

They say that every good story has a beginning, a middle, and an end. I have divided my story into three similar sections, but with a simple change. The truth for me is that once the diagnosis had been made, the story of Adrienne's cancer will never really be over. There will always be more tests, more vigilance, more fear. More appreciation for every accomplishment she makes. More gratitude for her continuing presence on this earth. More sleepless nights. More holding her longer and closer than she likes to be held, knowing she will just let it be okay.

Being aware of all these things, I have decided that this story should be divided up like this.

The Beginning

The Middle

The End…

The End, dot dot dot.

And if you are reading this because your daughter who is too young has been diagnosed with breast cancer, please know that my heart goes out to you.

Author's Note

Somewhere in the middle of The End... of this story, the world was hit with a global disaster named Covid 19. The reader will see references to the impact the restrictions caused by governments trying to stop the spread of the virus had on Adrienne's life and mine. These reflections are in no way intended to suggest that our experiences were worse than those of families who lost a child or other loved one to this terrible illness. To anyone who had to go through that, please know I meant no disrespect by speaking of how it affected us, nor did I intend in any way to minimize your losses in relationship to mine.

My child is alive. I am very well aware that there is no comparison.

Table of Contents

12

The Beginning

The Lump

"By the way Mom, to keep you in the loop, I found a lump in the shower, so I followed it up with the doctor. She's sure it's nothing to worry about...probably a cyst... but she's sending me for an ultrasound next week. I mean, I'm only 27, right?"

"So, the ultrasound tech says definitely not a cyst because it's solid but she's sure it's just a fibroadenoma (the most common type of benign breast tumour)."

"Hey Mom...the doctor referred me to a surgeon because she thinks I should get a biopsy. I saw him and he's really nice and I still think it's okay because he's sure it's that fibro thing, too."

Then came the phone call...

"Mom...Mom...it's cancer."

If you have ever seen the short clip "Godzilla Versus Bambi" then you know what that felt like.

I pretty much went through the motions for the next couple of days. There were tasks that had to be accomplished in preparation for me going up to be with her for what was to come. I had no idea at the time what my life would look like in the ensuring months and in hindsight it's a very good thing I didn't.

One of the most difficult things was making the phone calls. I made sure that the people I love were not alone when they got the news. Something that I hadn't been able to do for my child, because everyone she dealt with during the investigational phase told her she was too young for it to be cancer. One of the biggest regrets of my life, having that much trust. I'm usually not an ostrich-head-in-the-sand type of person. I usually think through all the worst-case scenarios so that I am prepared. I have never been more unprepared in my life than I was for that phone call. Never has she been so unprepared to hear news. I think in part the fact that I didn't go there, literally or figuratively, gave her more confidence that it would be nothing. And it definitely wasn't nothing.

I was given a six month leave of absence from my job for which I am so grateful. I packed Spring, Summer and Fall into two suitcases (oh the agony of choosing which shoes to leave behind...first world problems) and moved across the country to live with her in her one-bedroom apartment while she underwent surgery and treatment.

And all of this because of...The Lump.

Shaving the Head

"Unfortunately there isn't a breast cancer chemo treatment where you don't lose your hair."

I wasn't able to be with Adrienne when she met the medical oncologist so she asked her friend Brian if he could come. I asked her if I could be on the phone on speaker so we could both hear the news at the same time and ask questions and the doctor welcomed that saying the more the better.

Some people end up with a special place in your heart. Her friend Brian now has a corner of mine.

The treatment news blew into the room like a hurricane when you're expecting maybe a gust or two of wind. The reasons for it were explained, questions asked and answered, all in all a very respectful exchange. Brian held her hand to give her human contact as the reality of the coming storm's ferocity smashed into her. And she held it together, I think allowing the scientist in her to be in control so she could get to the end in one piece.

Until he told her she was going to lose her hair.

Adrienne could be one of those heads you see in a style magazine in a salon. She's had long lustrous waving hair, red hair, one side shaved hair, bobbed hair, pixie cut hair, WTF WAS I THINKING hair...it's been a public expression of her emotions, her personality, her life.

And now her hair's absence was going to be a very public sign of something she still feels very privately about in many ways. That she is 27 years old and has cancer.

Fast forward a couple of weeks...after my arrival in Ontario.

"Mom, I think I'm going to call the salon and get my hair cut tomorrow. I keep looking at it, thinking it won't happen to me but it's just making it harder".

I walked into her room a little while later, frozen in place as I watched her run her fingers through her beautiful hair that just gotten to the perfect length after a year of working on it, tears running down her face. I held her as she wept. answering my question with of course, Mom, I want you there.

She actually needed me there, to help her get in and out of the hair washing chair because she was three days post surgery to take more tissue out of her breast. I made eye contact with her stylist over my little girl's head as she pushed back tears at what this haircut meant for the person sitting in her chair. I am severely allergic so after I while I had to go wait in the car because the stylist has a home salon and has cats.

I kept looking over my shoulder, checking in the rear-view mirror for her, thinking about what I would say. About fifteen minutes later I saw my daughter come out, and instead of the cute pixie cut she went in for, she has shaved her head.

"I was sitting there Mom and thought...fuck it. Let's just do it. Can we go look for some scarves?"

Of course, honey. Whatever you want.

Whippin' Off the Wig

Adrienne got a human hair wig and was able to take it to her stylist last night to get it cut "a la her". She came home with smile that could have lit up a football stadium because seriously, it's so perfect and you could never tell it wasn't her own head of hair. She needed to wait until she found some heat protection product to work with it at home but she found some hiding in her Stash of Any Hair Care Product Needed by Any Human Being to Create Any Style on Earth or Any Planet or to Infinity and Beyond and came to poke me about a half hour after we went to bed to show me.

IT LOOKS AMAZING!!!

Today we had a couple of appointments at the same hospital, one at 10:30 and one at 2:30, and she decided to wear her newly acquired OMG IT'S AMAZING wig. We had a few things to pick up and there was a mall about a twenty-minute walk away so we thought it would be fun and good for both of us to walk there between and have lunch.

An important piece of info for you to have to understand what transpired at the mall is that she started the hormone shots on Tuesday to stimulate egg production so they can retrieve them before chemo starts.

Fast forward to walking through the mall...on our way back after having lunch and picking up the above-mentioned few things.

"Is it hot and stuffy in here Mom or is it just me?"

"I'm good honey so I think it's just you."

"Can we stop to get me a bubble tea on the way back? I really feel like I could use a special lift and that kind of treat sounds perfect."

Of course we can.

As we were waiting for the tea to be prepared...

"Mom I don't think I can handle the hot and itchy I'm feeling from the wig right now. I don't want to just stuff it in a bag though, because it'll get squished."

"Hmmmmm...hey wait! Adrienne how about we put it in the compost buckets we just bought..that will protect it."

"Great idea Mom! I think I'm going to take it off. I brought my white scarf to cover my head so I think I'm gonna wear that this afternoon."

"Okay..I think there's a washroom about..."

Annnndddddd she whips off the wig. While waiting for a bubble tea. In the middle of a mall.

That's my girl.

Sisters

So, Isabelle came for a visit. And brought with her a wave of normal, that somehow perfectly blended in with our new normal.

She talked about plans with her friends. She talked about the boy. She talked about her job. She talked about milkshakes and how Tim Horton's new Take on a Shake is alright but kind of watery. She talked about laughing at totally inappropriate moments when she went to see Les Miserables last weekend in Los Angeles with another person who has a corner of my heart (you know who you are David Kim), something that we were supposed to do together on Mother's Day but I was...otherwise engaged. She talked about her Wizard in League of Legends (I have no idea but apparently, it's a big deal).

Adrienne showed her the wig and talked about styling the hair. She brought out the scarves and head covers she's picked up and demonstrated the cool ways she's learned to tie them from YouTube (at which point Isabelle very clearly pointed out that she could look at YouTube videos for months and still have no idea how to do it). Adrienne talked about what's gone on so far with appointments and explained some of the procedures and how it's much busier than she had expected. She offered her opinion when asked about some of the changes Isabelle is contemplating making in her life. She talked about their shared phone plan and how they're going to try to play the Cancer Card to get the phone company to waive the rest of the money owing on the one she has so she can get a new one and give the old one to Isabelle (which will be a big deal because Isabelle is about 57 versions behind).

At one point Adrienne asked me to check if her left arm was swollen. She had been told to watch for lymphedema, which

22

is where lymph fluid doesn't drain properly after surgery on the lymph nodes, which she had had the week before. I got up and stood in front of her on the couch, closing my eyes and putting my hands around each of her upper arms so I could use my sense of touch to feel if there was a difference in size. They were sitting beside each other on the couch and when I opened my eyes, they were looking at me like I was nuts.

"Are you trying to cast a spell or something, Mom? Because that's what it looks like. I keep waiting for you to chant."

And we laughed. We laughed so hard.

I sat in my spot in the corner of the couch (Sheldon Cooper has NOTHIN' on me) and watched the wonder of sisterhood. Laughed with them as they made gentle loving fun of me a few more times. Marveled at how these two women, who are SO different, connect with each other in such an inexplicably miraculous way.

So hear me all those who wield Zhonya's Hourglass to Defend and Destroy on the Fields of Justice. Your Wizards may have great strengths, but they have absolutely no power over the magic of...

Sisters.

Silver Linings

This morning was an early one...4:15 am for me to be at the hospital at 6:45 for day surgery to insert a Portacath (I'm old and I need the caffeine to kick in so I don't kill someone like a poor hospital volunteer just trying to give me directions). For those of you who have no experience with cancer a Portacath is a way to provide chemo more easily for someone with Diamond Level numbers of treatments and since Adrienne has always been a high achiever...

There was no call confirming the appointment as there has been with everything else she's done and Adrienne had a mini panic attack in the car that we were going to the wrong hospital and sure enough, we were. I think maybe she's psychic which is terrifying because I still have a few secrets from her and I may have to clear my head (STAY PUFT MARSHMALLOW MAN) whenever she is near.

Sooooo off we went to the other hospital and got her registered, changed into the newest addition to her style collection...she looks so lovely in blue...and found our way to the surgical waiting room.

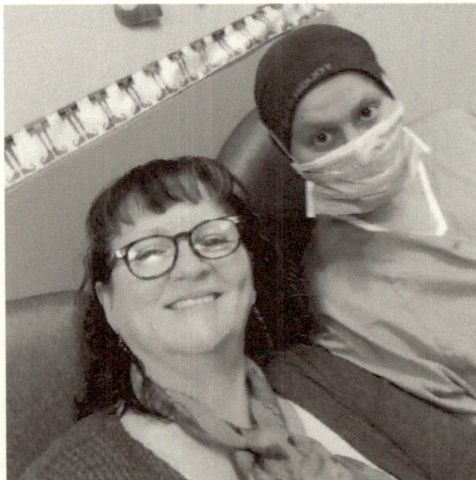

The only other people in the room were an older man and his son. Let me preface this by assuring you that this tale is told with gratitude, respect and affection, because a gift they were to us this morning when nerves were already frayed.

Imagine, if you will, watching a Monty Python skit where a son is trying to explain to his father how his flip phone works.

"Just press the green button Dad. It's all set up with my number. I'm the only one in your contacts."

"How will I know it's you?"

"Because I'm the only one in your contacts, Dad."

"How do I answer if it rings?"

"Just open it up if it rings and we'll be connected, Dad."

"So I open it up and press the green button?"

"No Dad, you just open it up."

"Then why do I need to press the green button?"

"If you want to call me you need to press the green button Dad."

"Where is the green button?"

"You have to open the phone to see the green button, Dad."

"Okay I got it. If the phone rings I open it up and press the green button to call you."

"Dad..."

And now for something completely different...

"Here's all your pills, Dad. You'll need to bring those with you when you go in."

"Where's my hearing aid pill?"

"Dad you don't take a pill for your hearing aid."

"Yes I do. I need one to help me pee then one for my hearing aid."

"Dad you don't need a pill for your hearing aid to work."

"Yes I do. It's a round thing I use for my hearing aid. I need one to pee and one to hear."

"Dad...that's the battery."

Under the category of everything happens for a reason, if we'd been at the other hospital, we would have missed all that.

Silver linings...

In the Beginning

In the beginning, it was just a lump.

Then it became a little bit of cancer (is that like being a little bit pregnant?) that they were going to go in there and take out along with a few lymph nodes to see if some of that little bit of cancer had seen a new neighbourhood and decided it was time to move on up (depending on how she's standing potentially to the east side...if you're old like me you'll get that reference). The hope was that once the lump was gone, she'd no longer be the girl with cancer.

Then hearing the news that one of the lymph nodes taken out during the surgery "looked a bit suspicious" so she went from the girl who didn't have cancer because the lump was gone to the girl who maybe had cancer. That waiting game, waiting to find out the results of the tests, is seriously enough to drive you to drink. Which I did. Not to excess, mind you, but to stay in my skin.

People say live in the moment. Don't worry about what you can't control as you go through your day to day. To all of you who say that when someone is waiting to hear whether or not they or someone they love still has cancer I say...go fuck yourself.

Then going to see the surgeon for the post-op checkup and hearing the glorious news that the lymph nodes were cancer free. That the report said the margins weren't fully clear but that he knew they were because he'd gone in to get some more tissue before he closed up. So, she was the girl who didn't have cancer. That kind of news is also enough to drive you to drink. Which we did. Not to excess, mind you, but to do something with the massive amounts of fight or flight hormones that were raging in our bodies as we prepared to hear that the cancer had spread. Because trust me, you need to be prepared.

Then meeting with the radiation oncologist who when going over the pathology report was a little concerned and wanted to get a second opinion on the margins. As a result, a second surgery is scheduled to go back in to take more breast tissue to test, so now once again the girl who maybe has cancer.

Funny how quickly that test result came back...no cancer cells in the extra breast tissue taken. Once again, the girl who doesn't have cancer. That kind of news can drive you to drink but we were so exhausted from all that other things she's dealing with that we just hugged each other and went back to watching Parks and Recreation. On the "seriously?" side, however, the torture we experienced the first time waiting for results is clearly not absolutely necessary. To a system that can generate speedier results so people don't have to agonize for weeks to find out if they still have cancer I say...go fuck yourself.

Then the surgeon saying that the radiation oncologist is also not happy about how one of her lymph nodes looks and although he wanted the surgeon to go in and take them all out he'll settle for a needle biopsy. The surgeon knows that patients who have the more aggressive surgery go through a lot of pain and recovery time and doesn't want her to go through that if she doesn't have to, especially since it will set her chemo back by six weeks to allow for healing. The biopsy is scheduled so once again, the girl who might have cancer.

At home after getting the Portacath inserted in what can only be described as a traumatic experience...to those of you involved in that particular "minor' surgical procedure, if I ever find out where you live...and the phone rings.

The biopsy was positive. My precious daughter is once again the girl with cancer.

Watching the blood drain out of her face. Quickly moving to her to provide support as she forces back the tears so she can try her best to participate in the conversation, the radiation oncologist asking questions about what kind of chemo was already scheduled and telling her that because they were already going after it so aggressively nothing will change except now she's looking at more surgery after it's done.

Sitting there helplessly raging at the universe because this is my little girl and I would do anything if I could wave a magic wand and make this all go away.

Then amazingly, watching her posture change. Seeing the power flow back into her, the defeat of the morning's experience replaced by determination, by the take-charge attitude that she has fueled herself on while navigating this ever-changing road.

"You know, Mom, at least now I know that all the things I'm going to go through are not preventative. If I ever have doubts that it's worth it I'm going to know it is. And you know what? I'm gonna kick this cancer's ass."

So to all the cancer cells trying to hide out in the darkness, waiting for a chance to come into the light, to establish a forward operating base in this war she's fighting, I have one message for you. Go fuck yourselves.

The Hatchening

You know, Hollywood has not prepared any of us for the actualities of cancer. There are the things we "know", such as chemo can cause hair loss and nausea and vomiting, but there are so many things we don't know until someone we love is faced with a cancer diagnosis...like the fact that chemotherapy drugs to treat breast cancer can cause infertility, either by throwing the patient into irreversible menopause or by damaging the reproductive system, in particular a woman's eggs.

For women in their forties or fifties, this might not be at the top of the worst side effects possible list. For a twenty-seven-year-old who is still in self-reflective exploration of whether or not children are in her future, it's like...WHAT?

An option given to cancer patients is something called Fertility Preservation, which involves going through fertility treatments so that eggs can be retrieved and frozen for future use. It's such a gift because with all that cancer takes from someone, this procedure means it doesn't get to take away the ability to become a biological parent. Adrienne basically decided not to decide right now if she wants to have a baby, so the call was made and off to the fertility clinic we went.

And went...and went...and went and went and went and WENT.

Unlike cancer, Hollywood has done a better job of preparing us for the wild ride of fertility hormone meds. These are not pretty little pink and blue pills you can swallow with a glass of wine over dinner as you peruse the latest sustainable and made with 175% recycled materials nursery furniture at BabiesCostaLot.com. These are shots...with needles...that you have to give yourself...in your belly...at the same time every single day sometime between 6 pm and 9 pm. And the needles contain hormones...crazy making lady hormones...the kind of crazy making that can be used as a defense in a court of law. The kind that make you weep if you drop a bit of bubble tea on your dress.

The first time, Adrienne asked me to do it because, as she said, it's against one's nature to stab oneself, in the belly or anywhere else. After one try at it and MOM DON'T TURN THE NEEDLE she decided to take that particular task on herself. First it was one shot. Then it was two or sometimes three because the dosage was two thirds of a pre-filled injector pen. On top of which a couple of pills to help control the estrogen surge that happens during these treatments since her cancer is estrogen receptor positive and we don't want to feed THAT particular beast.

The chemo that could cause Adrienne to become infertile was scheduled to start fifteen days after the first hormone shots started so she had one cycle to make this work. The clinic is in downtown Toronto and Adrienne lives almost in Pickering (GoogleMaps my friends). To see how the treatment is working patients have to go to the clinic between 7 and 8:45 am for a blood test and an ultrasound and a meeting with a nurse and they were able to (THANK GOODNESS) give her one of the later slots so we could sleep in until 5:30 to get on a 7 am commuter train to connect with a subway to be there on time. The results of the blood work tell you when you go in next. Sometimes that's in three days, sometimes that's in two days, sometimes that's tomorrow. Even if you have to figure out how to be at two appointments at the same time you have to go in. Even if you had surgery five days before the treatment starts and you're still having difficult walking around you have to go in because the process is so delicate that if things are just a bit off they have to cancel and start again. And Adrienne doesn't have time to start again.

During the ultrasound the technician rattles off numbers. At first, Adrienne wasn't sure what that was but as it turns out it's measurements of follicle development, which means eggs maturing, and they count those little individual miracles in both ovaries. As each successive ultrasound happened Adrienne developed, in her sister Isabelle's words, fish numbers of eggs. Her ovaries which are normally the size of an almond had grown to tennis ball sized by the time the decision was made to give the final shot which would cause the release of the eggs so they could be retrieved and frozen. The kick-it-in- gear shot (they call it a trigger shot, the only time you can use the words trigger and shot in the same sentence in a group of people and hear them shout WAHOO!!!) happened on Saturday, and the procedure happened this morning EXACTLY 36 hours from when that shot happened. Did I mention it's a delicate process?

And the results are already in...

Twenty eggs (yup Isabelle, fish numbers). She has twenty chances of having a child that will look like her, dance like her, master Ikea directions like her, yell WTF ARE YOU DOING DUDE like she does on the 401 freeway (maybe you should drive while I'm taking these hormone shots, Mom). Twenty chances to see herself in someone else, to see her child's spirit grow so much more powerful than her own, the way I am getting to every day right now. Twenty chances to raise someone bigger...badder...better.

Look out world..The Hatchening (© Isabelle Legault 2019) was a success!

About the Rest of Them

When I was pregnant with Adrienne, I thought…

"How will I love another baby as much as I love Stephanie?"

And then she arrived, and the love was just…there. With Isabelle I thought…

"I know I will love her, because I've done this before, and my heart grew two sizes to make room for all the love that happened the instant Adrienne took her first breath, so I know it will grow two sizes for Isabelle, too."

Is this what people are referring to when they say someone has a very big heart…hmmmmm?

We all know as parents that you're not supposed to have a favourite, and I don't. What I have come to realize lately, though, is that I do have a kid pyramid that's sort of like a Rubik's Cube that gets twisted and clicked until the colour of the one whose life is biggest at the moment ends up at the top. And cancer is REALLY REALLY big (there's a reason they call is the Big C and it has nothing to do with the latest porn phenom). It's all consuming in ways that I can't quite describe and don't think anyone who hasn't been where I am could fully understand. I certainly never would have.

Some very big things have happened in my other children's lives since the moment I first heard "Mom…it's cancer."…some REALLY REALLY big things that in other circumstances would have had me twisting and clicking away, the colour at the top of my kid pyramid changing. Sometimes because of pride, sometimes because of worry, sometimes because of excitement, sometimes because of apprehension, sometimes just because. But since that phone call on March 15th, no matter how many times I click and twist, only one colour ends up on top.

I have written a lot about how much admiration I have for Adrienne and how she is moving beyond any realm of strength and courage than I thought was possible in someone so young. How I have watched her take control of things she can and find ways to work through what she can't to see how it's going to help her beat the monster. And all of those things are true.

What is also true is how much pride I am experiencing right now in my other children. How much awe and gratitude I have for them as we meander down this road. How they are allowing me to hold their sister a little tighter without being envious, how they are not resenting me for not being able to do as much as I would normally do to celebrate their successes or hold their hands when their lives take an up or down turn. How they are stepping into roles that I would usually play because I either don't have the time or I haven't slept in days and I just can't. How they are just...there.

So, to all the rest of them, my heart that has already grown so many sizes is once again expanding to allow for what I'm feeling for you. You are amazing...you are magnificent...you lift me up.

You are so so so loved.

The Middle

Peeing All Three Primary Colours

Yes, colours...I'm back in Canada, eh.

Have you ever done something you really didn't want to do, put one foot in front of the other and moved forward while the voice in your head is screaming so loudly you're amazed that no one else can hear it?

That was me on Tuesday.

Up until now, everything that I have supported Adrienne through has been *because* of the cancer. The initial surgery...the hair...the second surgery...the biopsy...the Portacath...the fertility preservation...all *because* of the cancer. Imagine a period of time when the understudy has to take the lead role on stage because the star is busy in rehab...or golfing in Mexico...or in hiding because of a purported sex tape with a Muppet. The star is out there somewhere but not really in your face because you're so busy taking care of the understudy.

On Tuesday, I walked with Adrienne for the first time into the oncology ward at the hospital for the pre-treatment before chemo started on Wednesday. For the first time the star of the show was front and center ready to take the stage. Tuesday wasn't *because* of the cancer...Tuesday was *about* the cancer. And this particular show has a guaranteed twenty week run with 40 more in limited theaters.

Apparently, a part of me has still been in denial that this is actually happening. Some might say I was just living in the moment and only worrying about immediate needs. Thanks for giving me some credit but nope...spent the last three weeks floating on a barge in Egypt (get it?..I was in de-Nile) and this week the barge docked in Cancerville.

Wednesday was Chemo Day One. I packed us a lunch (I pack the coolest lunches, right David Kim?) because they recommended you do that when we went in for Chemo Teaching. We had entertainment options, warm socks (for Adrienne not for me...geez), and The Book which has all the questions Adrienne might have and a place to write down the instructions we need to remember, like the fact that one of the chemo drugs might make her pee red.

She asked me to take a picture of her to post on Facebook, joking that she was being a typical millenial who takes pictures of everything. I had to take a second one because the angle from the first one I took made her look like she had rolls (vanity thy name is woman...even if thou art afflicted). Here she is...

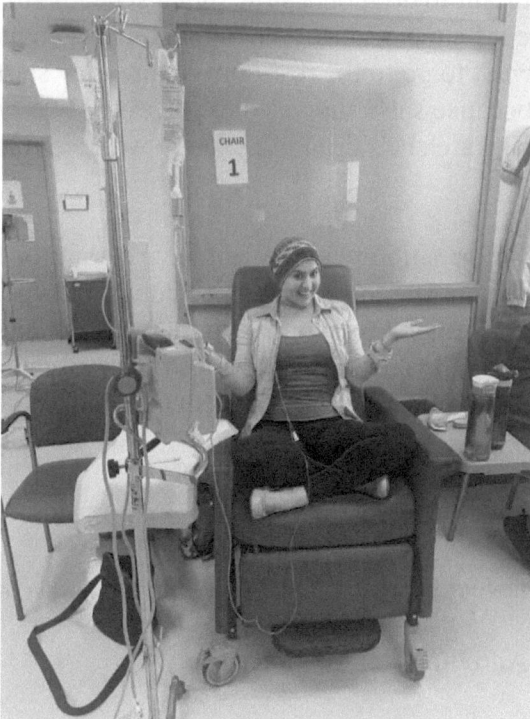

We side-eyed someone who came in wearing a hoodie and sunglasses and a hat to disguise themselves (dude, we all have cancer). She asked the nurse in charge of her, who is probably the same age as she is, how she got into oncology nursing.

And I sat there while they pumped toxins into my child.

She told me later she was impressed that I didn't even flinch. She's right, I didn't. Because the screams were so loud in my head that I was paralyzed.

There were two different chemo meds, a red one that had to be manually infused by the nurse and then a second one that would drip from an IV bag. They have to be very careful because the first one can actually burn the skin if it leaks out so it's important to do it on a slow timed schedule to ensure it goes where it's supposed to. When that one was done Adrienne went to go to the restroom before they started the other one because she's supposed to pee every two hours so she's making sure she's drinking enough water to make that happen.

A piece of information you may not have is that for the initial surgery in March she was injected with a blue dye to light up the sentinel lymph nodes so they could clearly identify them and take them out for pathology to check for cancer. As the dye cleared her system, she peed blue for a half a day.

She comes out of the restroom and looks at me and says

"Hey Mom...I've officially peed in all the primary colours".

Why yes, Adrienne, yes you have.

Who's the star of the show now, cancer?

Side Effects May Include...

Living in the United States for all these years I've seen more commercials than I can count suggesting patients talk to their doctors about new drug ZYWXV, the miraculous new treatment for (fill in the blank) that will change your life. Couples in side by side bathtubs watching the sun set, men who now have sexy elbows, women who can stop worrying about peeing themselves in public. All of these warm fuzzy moments for the poor souls whose lives were a *disaster* before ZYWXV.

Ah yes...then comes the disclaimer.

Potential side effects may include...the skin on your left baby toe turning a strange shade of magenta, everything you eat tasting like kale, urges to trot through malls smacking two coconuts together, spontaneous yodeling at all red lights, your right arm uncontrollably slapping people who ask you stupid questions...you get the picture.

Enter chemotherapy. And the drugs used to help with chemotherapy. And the drugs used to help the drugs used to help with chemotherapy. I mean, toxic sludge that is so powerful it can burn your skin being injected into you is one thing, but shouldn't that be the extent of what you have to worry about? We are giving you chemotherapy drugs to kill your cancer but hey, you have to watch out for blood clots. We are giving you something to help up your immune system but hey, your bones may feel like they're exploding. We're giving you something to help with the vomiting but hey, it may give you diarrhea.

Unfortunately for Adrienne, her mother (me) thinks it is much better to do research so you are prepared for as many eventualities as might arise from any given situation. So, I'm pretty up to speed about all the side effects that come with the multitudes of things she's been injecting, or swallowing, or rubbing on her skin, or having injected into her over the last two months. And so I watch, creepy stalking kidnapper body snatcher watch, every single move she makes. And I listen, the little hairs in my ears perking up like the Toy Story aliens listening for THE CLLLAAAWWWW at every sound she makes.

I'm trying very hard not to drive her crazy.

I don't know if she's noticed yet. We do a pretty good job of living together where each of us goes to our own corner when the introvert inside just needs some space. We've developed an excellent rhythm if we're in the kitchen together, doing a choreographed dance as we move from stove to sink and back again.

But I will admit, since she's gotten used to using her right arm for things because of the surgeries on her left side to treat the cancer, I analyze my questions for their stupidity factor before I ask them. Because potential side effects may include...

You get the picture.

I Still Believe in Magic

Adrienne and I are connected in a very Island JuJu kind of way. When I am far away from her, I will get a sense, pick up the phone and say…

"Hey Adrienne, how are you?"

And she'll say .

"MOM YOU'RE A WITCH"

Mostly because something will be going on that she really needs to talk to her Mommy about. For those of you worried about her calling me a witch it's a Glenda the Good Witch kinda thing because if she meant it in the bad way I'd squish her like a bug.

You can imagine what that connection is like when I'm sleeping 20 feet away from her.

This is chemo week and today is Monday, which is grocery shopping day for the things that seemed to be okay last time that we hope will still appeal to her at the end of the week. That means tomorrow is Tuesday, which is pre-treatment day. Which means that the day after that is Wednesday, when the toxins will once again flow into her veins. The last time there was anxiety because of the unknown. Now there is anxiety because of the known, and in this case, it's just a little bit worse to know, to watch them push the syringe, attach the IV, knowing exactly how shitty she's going to feel afterwards.

I was sitting on the couch today feeling the blood pump through my veins, feeling my throat slowly but surely tighten, feeling my stomach doing somersaults, and as I usually do, I started to reflect on where I was at. I was

41

feeling anxious about this week, yes, but the degree of physical reaction I was having was very intense for the actual level of my emotional state. So hmmmmm...

"Hey Adrienne...are you feeling anxious at all?"

"Yeah Mom I'm not having a good day at all. I'm so sorry, Mom. I know you pick up on it."

"That's okay babe...that's really okay."

Island JuJu at work. But...

On Saturday the weather was nothing less than spectacular, a very welcome change from the cold, miserable, wet, windy, MISERABLE weather we've been having. Ummmmm...well...actually in this household that crappy weather hasn't been all that bad, because chemo sucks and when you don't have the strength to get up off the couch to do more than go pee, looking outside at grey and wet makes it way easier to crawl back under the blanket on the couch and watch repeats of Gilmore Girls for the thirty-eight time. It really does.

Where was I? Oh yeah, Saturday.

This first four cycles of treatment is once every two weeks, and Adrienne asked me to stay with her for the entire first cycle (instead of going up north to see the grandbabies and the adults that take care of them) because neither of us knew how it was going to play out in week two, and week one was not fun at all. By Saturday, though, she was feeling pretty perky, so the decision was made to dress up a little bit and go on an adventure.

She looked beautiful...a sun dress, her new gorgeous wig, makeup applied to perfection. I looked

42

alright..whatever...and we took the train to Danforth to walk down the street to visit the funky little stores that are found there and then moved on to Kensington Market to do the same. We stopped to sit on a patio for a beer. We both found some amazingly cool pants that were cheap enough to buy and to celebrate. There were places I couldn't go into that sold hand made soaps and essential oils because my nose was NOPE and places that had incense burning in them she couldn't go for the same reason. There was sun and a lovely breeze and we were walking in and out of the clothing stores (who the heck would wear THAT?) and wandering into vintage stores (do you have any idea what THIS is?) and for a moment...for a precious golden moment...it was just me and my girl. The third wheel whose name starts with C and rhymes with dancer faded just enough into the background that it was just me and my girl.

So yes, I still believe in magic...and if I can have moments like that, to hold onto, where we connect in laughter and joy, I'll take the Island JuJu anytime.

Do You Have Any Chicken?

I started hosting a New Year's Eve fondue party pretty much as soon as my children were old enough to understand that tossing Barney the purple dinosaur across the room in a game of keep away was not a safe thing to do when there are open flames on the table (pre electric pots...I'm old). The main ingredient to the fondue is very thinly sliced beef that can be wrapped around cheese and cooked to perfection in a delicious broth. A long time ago in a world very different from the one I am living in now, my friends who had been with us several times over the years for the event in Canada were driving from home to Detroit to fly down for a visit in California over the holidays and were going to be with us once again for New Year's Eve.

To protect the guilty, I will call them Mennis and Darilyn.

I tried everywhere I could think of close to my home to get that beef but alas, it was not to be. Something to do with health regulations and slicers...whatever. I was racking my brain trying to come up with an alternative and when Darilyn asked me in a phone conversation close to departure time if she could bring anything I jokingly said "Yeah, if it weren't for the border crossing you could bring the meat". And then our minds started to work, which if you know us can be a scary thing for the rest of our family members. You could put it frozen in your luggage with some ice packs... it's winter, the luggage will stay cold. It's not like you're bringing a case of Kinder Eggs. Worst case scenario you play the dumb card and they take it away.

Challenge accepted.

Mennis has crossed the border more times that he can count and has the Q and A part of the exercise down to a science. You're respectful and you answer the questions exactly as asked, giving no more or no less information than is actually asked for. So here's how it went...

"Where are you going?"

"To fly out of Detroit to visit friends in California for the holidays."

"How long are you staying?"

"Seven days?"

"Do you have any cigarettes or alcohol?"

"No, sir."

"Do you have any chicken?"

Do you have any chicken. I cannot imagine what was going through the border crossing guard's mind, nor how Mennis kept his face straight when he honestly answered, knowing he had four pounds of illegal beef in his luggage...

"No, sir, I do not have any chicken."

"Have a nice time in California." *stamp stamp drive away*

So why, in my story about my experience of my daughter's cancer experience, am I telling you this story?

Because as I have stated before, cancer is an all-consuming beast that permeates every second of every minute of every hour of every day of your life. There have been golden moments and I'm sure there will be more, but even those are measured against all the rest of the moments that are filled with fear, and anguish, and anger, against the times when I'm screaming silently, when I shed the hidden tears that only a mother can shed.

I remember when I went to work at the library one of the best things was having stories to tell, to bring funny or odd moments to my conversations with people both inside my family and out. Stories that were mine to own and to share. And they were about different things every week, what my kids were doing, adventures I was having, they caught them having sex WHERE in the stacks? My world got bigger with my job, and I took such joy in my day to day interactions with everyone involved.

My world has gotten much smaller in the last few months, the focus of my attention narrowing, all of my energy going into supporting Adrienne in the biggest battle she has ever fought, and believe me this is not the first time in her life she's been to war. And as a result, my stories are different, yes, but they're really all about the same thing.

And so now, when people are asking me about how things are, how I'm doing, how's she doing, is there anything new, I need to take a minute to think about how exactly I should respond. Do you have the need to be in the circle of information? Do you have the inner strength to hear what this is really like without putting up a protective barrier to stop yourself from thinking about your own mortality, or hers? Do you really want the truth?

Do you have any chicken?

Dumpster Diving, Anyone?

Today Adrienne and I did our own version of dumpster diving...but I'll get back to that later.

When Adrienne was younger, you pretty much needed a backhoe to get across the room from her door to her bed (like mother, like daughter). Granted she was very busy with school and dance classes and later work and work and WORK and school, so it's very necessary to cut her some slack. We had a rule about keeping the common area clean and clear of debris because I could always shut her door, and as an adult living in her own space, now that she only has one job (thank you universe) she has adopted that rule and EVERYTHING in the common area - bathroom, living room, kitchen - has it's place. She takes a great deal of pride in her home and makes sure that it shines, especially when someone is coming over. Cushions match curtains match wall decor...it's actually a pretty snazzy pad.

I have noticed over the last few weeks, however, since chemo started, and even more the last few days since chemo treatment number two, that she doesn't complete things. It's pretty funny, actually. She'll walk into a room knowing exactly what she wants to do, do part of it, then SQUIRREL. For example, one of her pet peeves is cupboards being open, and this morning she opened a cupboard to look for something, pulled a box a bit of the way out of the space to check behind it, and when she didn't find what she was looking for just stood up and walked away to look somewhere else. Now I KNOW if the fog lifts and she walks back into the room and sees that it will drive her nuts, so I started chuckling and pushed the box back in and closed the door. And before you tell me I would never have done that when she was a kid, that I would have made it a teachable moment, if she'd had cancer as a kid you can bet I would have. I can't do anything to fix the cancer, but I can do a lot to make her life easier by fixing the little things.

Today we were sitting outside knowing it was her last few hours of feeling decent enough to do so before the side effects take over when she looked at me and said...

"Mom I think I recycled my vehicle registration and insurance card last week when I was cleaning up."

She was googling how to replace it, realizing it would mean a trip to Service Ontario, knowing that can't happen until next week because she won't feel up to it, worrying about us getting pulled over and not having the paperwork to produce when asked (fat chance because I'm driving like a granny but you never know). This is not something, unfortunately, that I could fix.

LIGHT BULB FLASHES ABOVE HER HEAD...

"Hey Mom when did I do that, last Wednesday right? The recycling hasn't been picked up yet, maybe it's still in there!"

I can tell, by the look on her face, that the realization that she has just suggested we go search through the huge recycling can that is shared with the two other parties that live in the house is sinking in.

"I'm so sorry, Mom."

"It's all good honey...let's go."

So...it's been nine days of other stuff being put in the bin. Nine days of cans, and pizza boxes, and plant containers and...other things. We're digging in, pulling out this and that, and there are papers on the very, very bottom that we can't reach (where were you, Isabelle, when we needed you most?) that she thinks might be it and I look at her and say "I think we have to dump it." This is a time you hope the neighbours are not being nosy...right? Seriously.

Bin dumped, a pile of papers and other stuff pulled out, and a yelped...

"YES YES YES YES YES!!!"

Because there it is, in all its glory. THE PLASTIC ZIPPER BAG SPECIALLY DESIGNED FOR KEEPING PAPERWORK SAFE IN A CAR WITH ALL THE DOCUMENTS INSIDE.

All this time I'm thinking it's some loose papers that just got mixed up with some flyers and junk mail but noooooo. It's a very obvious "YOU SHOULD NOT PUT THIS IN THE RECYCLE BIN BECAUSE THERE ARE IMPORTANT THINGS INSIDE" bag. And all I can do is laugh because what else are you supposed to do when your very organized, smart daughter does something so (insert adjective here) because chemo has her in its foggy grips?

"Wait a minute, Mom, I think I might have put something of Isabelle's in there with all her personal information on it"

Adrienne is no longer allowed to recycle unsupervised.

Motherhood

This was a weird weekend.

Adrienne asked me to stay with her for the whole first cycle of her chemo since there was no playbook to know how she'd feel on any given day. As it turns out, the last few days before chemo cycle two were actually pretty good and it was decided that if she felt the same way the next time I'd head up to Barrie to be with the rest of the family for the last little while before it started again.

"Mom please get outta my house for a few days so I can have it to myself. I mean I love ya and all but...yeah"

Since I arrived back in Ontario on May 7th, we have not been apart for more than a few hours. I've been by her side for painful procedures, blood draws, giving herself shots (MOM DON'T MOVE THE NEEDLE...I'll never live that down), stitches itching and being removed, good news and bad, tears and laughter, toxins being pumped into her. I've been sad, I've been angry, I've been frustrated, I've been paralyzed, but through all of that I have kept the fear at bay because, well, there were things to do. And she was right there within reach of my arms if she needed anything.

This past Thursday afternoon was my grandson Elliott's preschool graduation and I really wanted to go but Adrienne wasn't quite ready to be on her own yet and she really loves that little boy so she came up with me. The biggest issue this chemo round was headaches...miserable, pounding, going to sleep with waking up with headaches (Mom can you please massage my head again?) and as a result she was very noise sensitive. If you've been in a house with a four year old boy and a fifteen month old girl you'll be very aware that quiet isn't really an achievable goal, and so Isabelle offered to stay with us to free up her apartment so Adrienne could stay there

50

and get some rest. The apartment is five minutes from Stephanie's (one of the grownups who takes care of my precious grandchildren) so if something happened and she needed me it was a short drive to go to her.

Five minutes away felt like she was in another universe beyond where my arms could reach to catch her if she fell, literally or figuratively. The plan was if she felt good, she'd go home to Toronto on Saturday and I'd stay in Barrie until Monday. And she did. I lost my freakin' mind. As it turns out, I am afraid. So very, very afraid.

I have glimpsed the fear here and there, in the shadows. Felt it as fleeting touches like a breeze teasing the hair on the back of my neck. It has never been allowed to manifest, until this weekend. And when it did, it ate me alive. It made my heart race. It made me feel and act frantically. Filled up the space inside of me with a savagery and suddenness that I was not prepared for. It turns out that I have this irrational mindset that if I'm with her nothing more bad will happen. I can't do anything to protect her from the creature inside her, but I can and will do everything in my power to keep her safe from invaders from without. Like I'm some Marvel character or something (sorry, not sorry DC Universe). When she slept at Isabelle's I wasn't there. When she came back to Toronto I wasn't there. And the fear sat on my shoulder, whispering in my ear…

"Who is guarding her now?"

Now I'm back in Toronto because the cycle starts again tomorrow. She is rightfully a little sad that she has lost her aloneness again. Cancer has taken away her independence, and she's always been fiercely independent (like you were, Mom). We both know that in a couple of days she's going to feel like crap and she'll be very glad I'm here, but for today it's like a battle lost, not because she's not fully engaged in the war, but because she has had to accept that this particular one she can't win. That's part of what my re-entry represents.

As for me, I'm breathing again. I felt the fear receding with each stop along the train ride. I pushed it back into the netherworld and closed the portal as soon as I saw her. I'm here, guarding her, protecting her, keeping her safe. Do I know that this makes me sound a little crazy? Sure, I do. But I can state with certainty that regardless of what you think, sometimes there is nothing quite so delusional as...

Motherhood

Relativity Has Different Lenses

I have often said that everything is relative, and I truly believe that it is. I have a roof over my head, I have food to eat, I have clean water to drink, so relative to someone who has none of those things I live a dream existence. I have always worked very hard to "see" my life, how fortunate I have been, how well choices I have made have worked out for me.

I am sitting beside my child, and I am able to do that without worrying that my bills will get paid, so relative to someone who could not make that choice I am very fortunate.

I have people who love and support me, who I know would drop everything and come if I asked them to, so relative to people who are alone in the world I am very fortunate.

I am able to see my grandchildren often, so relative to grandparents who can only do that once a year, or whose grandchildren are on another continent, or who don't have grandchildren to visit, I am very fortunate.

But relativity indeed has different lenses, and the fact that it took me quite a lot of thought to come up with those three things tells me a lot about what's colouring mine. At this moment I am looking at my life a little differently. Something is making it very difficult for me to see how lucky I am...relatively speaking.

Here's my emotional range this week so far. I'm trying to figure out how to replace the cheese flavoured Goldfish that I'm stress eating every night when I tuck myself into bed with something a little healthier (I dare you to think of something as ridiculously delicious). I'm trying not to be really pissed off that the computer version of Two Dots only has 760 levels and I have to start over AGAIN because I beat all of them. I am laughing very hard at Jo Koy on Netflix. That's relatively small and petty, right?

Before you judge, though, let me share my true emotional reality right now...my day to day reality. My child, who I would give my life for, has cancer. She's going to beat it, of that I am sure (don't I have to be?), but what she has to go through to do so is just...awful. I'm struggling with a lot of feelings that are fighting their way to the surface at very inopportune moments and this is how I do that.

I ponder Goldfish replacements, get mad a computer games, and watch stand up on Netflix. Anything to hold back the walls ready to crush me.

You know what? I have a new Theory of Relativity.

Emotions = Motherf&#@ing Cancer^2

Island Juju Part Deux

You know, I read on the internet that Canada is banning straight marriage during Pride Month, that Kelloggs is introducing a ranch flavoured Pop Tart (MMMMMMM), and that Round Three of chemo can kick the cancer patient's ass. And because I read it on the internet we all know those things must be true...right?

Guess which one of those won't make the fake news list on Snopes.com? And yes, I'm very well aware that I could have made a Trump joke because I used the term fake news, but then I would have had to misspell things by adding H's (Chanada, Pop Thart, and if you don't get the reference...Prince of Whales) and I couldn't bring myself to do it.

Ah round three. If all the world's an ice rink and we're all hockey players on it, I'd like to throw down my gloves and beat the shit out of you so we both have to go home (nice hockey reference there because I'm back in Canada, eh?)

One of the uplifting things that's been happening (and there are many believe it or not) is that far away people in Adrienne's life have been sending her care packages with all kinds of fun stuff in them. Stuff that clearly shows that a lot of thought, a lot of care, a lot of hope went into them. And a LOT of tape on the outside of them (Auntie Sandie did you think someone was trying to break into a vault?) a LOT of Ikea ziplock bags (hey thanks for replenishing my stock, Auntie Fran) and a LOT of sparkles (to make sure no one can dull mine, right Auntie Paula?).

And a LOT of love.

When she puts on a scarf, she says she can feel the love and support flow into her. The support of all the people who have come together to provide her with different and fun head coverings that she can learn to tie in new and funky ways from YouTube. Footnote...I still have no idea how she does it. I could watch those videos over and over and still end up looking like a tool.

When she wraps herself in her blanket she says she can feel the power of the love that went into making it wrapping her up and holding her closely when she needs it most, the hands carefully measuring and matching edges, cutting just so with the (DON'T TOUCH MY) sewing scissors, gently folding it so it will fit into a box.

When she looks at the sparkles she knows that someone out there still thinks she does, that despite all she's lost she hasn't lost that, the part of her that gives off light, that can bring a little bit of magic into a room, that allows her to surprise people who know but haven't seen her, who think she'll somehow have been dulled by this experience.

And when she feels those things, all that love and hope and care, reaching out to her across the miles, I get to feel them, too. Island JuJu at work in her is Island JuJu shared with me.

So, thank you. All of you. For giving me such a special gift.

Island JuJu...Part Trois – Can We Not Be So Connected Please?

This past weekend was the magic time for Adrienne, when she has a few days with minimal side effects from the chemo except, of course, for the bone deep fatigue...that one is ever present. My husband got here on Tuesday and we took the train up to Barrie on Friday to see the grandbabies and the other family members we have up there (that joke never gets old when you're a grandparent) which is a happy place for me. Adrienne had some VERY fun plans with her friends...very "her" summer things, like dressing up to go out to dinner and karaoke (with the IT'S AMAZING WIG), a trip to the lake for a sleepover and some water fun. The sorts of things that many 27 year old women would like to do, easy lighthearted pleasure things that come with laughter and friendship and create sunshine filled memories.

On Sunday night around 6:30, I went downstairs to pack up my suitcase because the latest train back to Toronto leaves at 7:18 am and Monday mornings are hard enough without scrambling to find your missing underwear or your toothbrush. I was just puttering around when I was overwhelmed by a deep, aching sadness, and I started to cry. I understand that I have lots of reasons to cry these days, but this one was completely out of the blue. And with it the thought came...

"I wish more of her weekends could be like this one."

At around the same time, Adrienne was on the road back from the lake. With every mile she drove she became more angry...more sad...more frustrated at how every second of every minute of every day of her life is impacted by cancer. With every mile she knew she was driving back into the darkness, because this is chemo week, and chemo sucks. While her friends are planning the next get-together for a birthday celebration, she is hoping that her next chemo will be better...they keep telling her it will be better...so that she can go, but as of right now she has no idea. And even if she can, cancer will keep her from doing some of what they do, from going some of where they go, from eating most of what they eat.

And all that emotion flowed into me in the basement in Barrie where I was packing my suitcase. And oh my goodness the wall of it I walked into when I got back here on Monday. She was trying so hard to contain it but it was too big...just, too big. I felt my throat tightening. I felt my heart racing. I wanted to run. And if that was how I was feeling, how bad was it for her? I've never felt so helpless in my life.

Before you doubt it, does she have a positive attitude? You bet she does. This is a battle and she is a warrior and she will win. On Sunday, however, she was just so angry. And on Monday angrier still. Because she's 27 years old and she has cancer. And that just isn't fair.

So it's a double-edged sword, this thing we have, and just for a moment yesterday when it was so very bad I thought...can we not be so connected please? But then I immediately took that wish back from the universe, and I'm so very glad I did. Because today she found a Spiderman camping chair for Elliott and she sprinkled me with the fairy dust of her joy at her discovery.

Thanks, Adrienne.

Real Talk...Chemo Sucks

So, Wednesday was Adrienne's last of the four chemo cycles that she has been told will be the hardest of what she'll have to do. They say that this particular cocktail's side effects are cumulative, meaning that with each cycle the afterwards is worse. They are very right.

This is my girl this week...

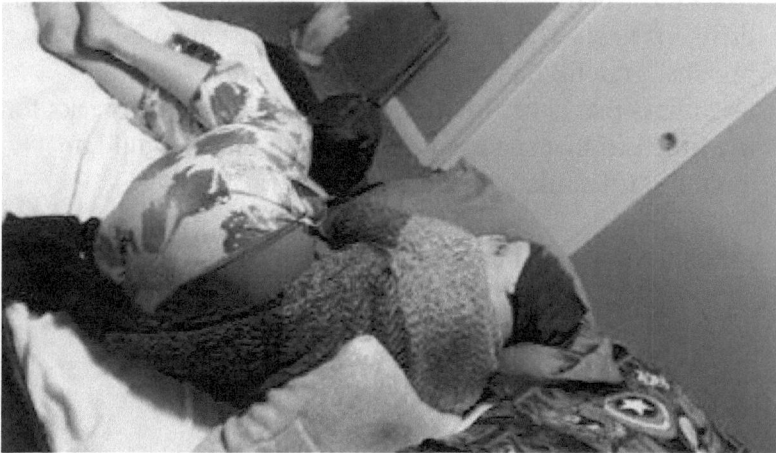

In previous cycles she's had a least a little bit of time when she felt semi-normal. This time she had to take some extra anti-nausea meds in the chair while the poison was going in. Last cycle we were able to go for a short walk every day. This time motion sickness kicks in getting from her bed to the bathroom. Her body hurts. Her lips are so pale we've been joking that they are lost somewhere in her bedding. This time there have been tears because she's so tired, and so tired of feeling this way.

We have a family vacation starting today an hour and a half down the road that's been in the planning for a year. We were really hopeful that she'd be feeling well enough today, like she did last cycle on the Saturday, for us to tuck her into the car and bring her there although her plan was just to sit in a chair with her feet up. Now we'll be lucky if she can make it tomorrow because this is hitting her like a sledgehammer. She's so disappointed. The only positive thing about it is the hope that the sledgehammer is doing the same thing to the cancer cells as it is to her.

She lays her head on my lap and I rub her head softly just like I did when she was a little girl. As with then, she often drifts off to sleep and I sit very quietly, listening to her breathe, grateful that she is getting a respite from the awfulness that is her life this week. And my heart breaks for my little girl that she has to go through this. I would do anything if I could somehow take it away.

Real talk, folks. Chemo sucks.

Two Bald Chicks at a Campground

We got to go! She wasn't feeling a lot better the next day, but she was bound and determined to do it and was feeling better enough to allow us to pack her into the car for the drive out to the lake. Better enough is a new norm for us as she encounters each day that comes managing the side effects of chemotherapy. It's a sad thing, all the new terms in our vocabulary. She drugged herself to the gills with all the anti-nausea chemo meds she had in her arsenal and we packed her with pillows and blasted the air conditioning all the way there.

This was the first time we had all been in the same place since treatment had begun. I can't imagine what it must have been like for all the other people who love her to see the impact, and I will never be more proud of them than I was with how none of what they must have been feeling was on their faces. The one common feeling was intense gratitude that she had been able to make it. No one said it out loud, but the words hovered over us the whole time we were there, little thought bubble clouds everywhere.

There was so much laughter in that week.

Poor Isabelle got "The Curse" and was bedbound for a day with cramping misery and Adrienne brought her some French fries in bed as she watched something on the tablet, the sort of big sister thing that she had done when they lived together in the university days. Such a normal thing for her to be able to do when her own body was managing misery of her own.

Adrienne floated at the pool and down at the lake, laughing with her nephew Elliott as he practiced swimming along side her and then nervously said "I don't want to do this" when he climbed on the floatie with her.

By the end of the week I had almost forgotten the pain of the week before. Watching her spend time with her family, teasing each other, by the end having the stomach to drink a few glasses of wine with her Dad, all of these things brought me such joy and relief after what had happened just a few days ago. Adrienne's cancer has been such a roller coaster ride and feeling such anguish on one day and such pleasure a few days later is example of why it's so crazy making. There were just so many little things that I probably wouldn't have noticed before that filled my heart up. My gratitude bubble soon ate up all the rest of them in its sheer magnitude and bathed us all in its warmth.

Adrienne had purchased camping chairs for both Elliott and his sister Clara, and this picture pretty much sums up the week.

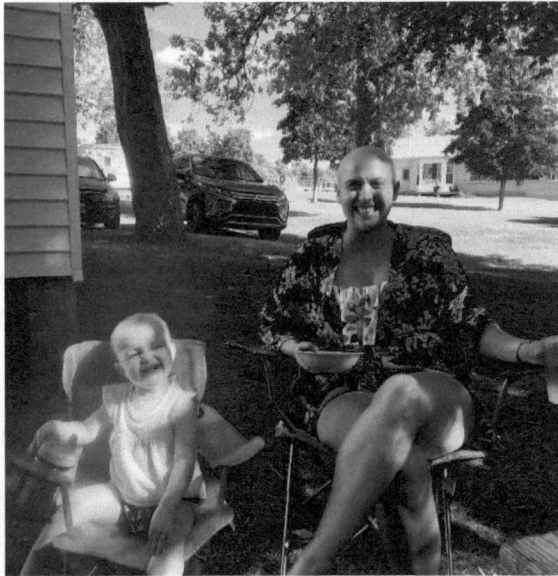

The caption for this photo could read...

Two Bald Chicks at a Campground. Nice, right?

Apparently We Have a Thing with Chicken

So today was the first day of the second round of chemo. This cycle will include two medications week one (Taxol and Herceptin), one medication weeks two and three (Taxol), two medications week four (Taxol and Herceptin) etc for twelve weeks with Herceptin continuing every three weeks for an extra forty weeks once the Taxol is done.

Are you confused yet?

We were at the hospital at 8 am this morning so that they could do a blood draw because they needed to make sure that she was fit to start the second cycle. Something about her liver working as it should (um we just came off vacation and there were a few elbows bent!) and her bone marrow having recovered (she stabby-stabbed herself even on vacation with the shots that are supposed to make that happen). Not surprisingly, it came back okay so the order was given to THE MAD SCIENTISTS (don't go in the door, children MUAHAHAHAHA) to formulate her chemo drugs. That takes a couple of hours and we didn't want to hang around but we had a great parking space, so we decided to walk to the mall to have some breakfast.

Side note...there must be several seniors' residences close to this particular mall because in the morning seniors are there en masse having coffee and tea and muffins and hogging all the tables in the food court as they socialize. Both Adrienne and I LOVE it! It's amazing to see them engage with each other and it's fun for us to try to figure out what they are talking about. Politics? Prostates? Pickles? Pierre who just moved into 3C?

After breakfast we walked back to the hospital and they were able to take us in early. They have had some issues with significant allergic reactions to Taxol so they jacked her up on IV Benedryl and IV steroids before they hooked her up. If you've ever had IV Benedryl you'll know you get sooo sllleeeeeepppyyyyyyy so she drifted off a couple of times while they were fussing then went out for the count just around the time they were going to start the Taxol drip. They had told her several times to let them know if she felt funny because they need to catch the allergic reaction early to...well...make sure she doesn't die. And I'm thinking hmmmmm...she's so snoozy so I'll keep an eye out for a reaction because I'm not sure she'd notice if she's out.

Second side note...Several years ago when there were members of my family in Japan, the Middle East, British Columbia, Ontario and California a group chat was begun to keep everyone connected. Even though geographic locations have changed and some of us are closer, we still use it to chatter about the important and the mundane and yes, because there are millenials in the group, we get pictures of food. During treatment all involved want to be updated about what's going on so I send the odd message like this one today...

Annnnddd the poisoning begins.

You know, because we are warped and twisted and I know they'll get it.

And this is where it went from there

Me
She's asleep so I'm watching to see if she grows hens

Me
HORNS!

Scott (Adrienne's brother in law)
Grow hens would be...interesting

Isabelle (Adrienne's sister)
I immediately pictured a chicken coming out of her chest Alien style

Me
BOCK BOCK BOCK visualizing blood flying off of feathers in all directions

Adrienne
I fall asleep for an hour and all of a sudden I've got demon chicken parasites?

Me
Yes. In your blood. Pac Man'ing all the cancer cells.

Luc (Adrienne's Dad)
Hahaha

Adrienne
That's an image haha

So yeah, apparently, we have a thing with chicken. And I'm okay with that. Especially after spending nine hours in the hospital watching the poisons flow.

Bock Bock Bock.

Waiting for the Other Shoe to Drop

Adrienne and I just got back from the hospital - today was her second round of chemo in cycle two, the Taxol. Two down, ten to go.

The first cycle, the every second week AC, had dreadful side effects that set in almost right away. Nausea, loss of appetite, bone deep fatigue, and generally just feeling like crap. The effects were cumulative and each cycle it got worse, until on the last one she barely got off the couch for three days. Everyone said the Taxol would be easier, and we were both hopeful that at least some of the body Hulk smashing she took with the AC would not be around for the twelve weeks of the second cycle. To be prepared, we had read all the material given to us about the potential side effects, and the medical oncologist was fairly sure that the nerve damage to her hands was a likely thing she'd encounter, and that other than that muscle aches are typical. Nausea was unlikely but possible.

Going into last week Adrienne experienced Anticipatory Nausea before the Taxol was started. This occurs in about twenty five percent of cases where body has a conditioned response, that chemo equals nausea, so nausea starts before the stuff is going in. She took some anti-nausea meds in the chair and it seemed to subside, and with all the other drugs they put in there she was passed out for most of the treatment anyway. And then the next day...

No nausea...none...zilch...zero...nada...NO NAUSEA. And she was HUNGRY...what?

Golden right? Yes but...

I made light and fun of a lot of things in this blog earlier on, but the reality is that the AC chemo cycle was REALLY bad. Like block it out and don't think about it bad. Like crying that she couldn't do twelve weeks like that with the Taxol bad. That it's a good thing that they found cancer because she didn't know if she could do this preventatively bad. So I have decided to give it a name, to wrap it up in a phrase that speaks its truth. Probably because I just binged Stranger Things. It shall forthwith be called The Awful.

And that brings us to now. Life this week has been very weird. The house is pulsating with anxiety, with sleeplessness, with frustration at the anxiety and the sleeplessness. Because the AC cycle has taught us one thing. That you have to be prepared. You can't go into it unless you're ready to experience the worst of it. You can't pretend it won't happen to you. You have to be ready to fight, have your armies on standby just in case. You have to have someone there in case you need help. You can't trust that you'll go to sleep okay and wake up okay. Every little ache, every little tingle in your fingers or toes, every little bit of lightheadedness, could mean that the worst of it is upon you.

So, we sit here, in this one-bedroom apartment, hiding from each other a bit, the memories of The Awful so close at hand. It is so big it almost has a physical presence, the fear of trusting, of letting it in. Because she feels good. She feels so very, very good.

Waiting for the other shoe to drop.

She Needs Me, She Needs Me Not

Sooooo it's been a while. I feel like I've been on the sidelines watching my life go by waiting for, as I said earlier, the other shoe to drop. And...well...it hasn't...sort of. There are some signs of the side effects we were warned about, and since Taxol is cumulative, they may get worse, but at present they are not enough to stop Adrienne from living most of her life. I say most of her life because right now the worst side effect is "Chemo Brain". She literally can't focus enough to do ANYTHING that requires multitasking. For that matter, sometimes she gets lost in the middle of a single task and stands there with a blank look on her face trying to get it back. Unfortunately, a lot of her job requires her to be able to flip back and forth between multiple documents so she's struggling with trying to work from home which she very much wanted to do. But she still feels so good. She's calling it "The Honeymoon" and her partner on the trip is normalcy that has, once again sort of, come back to her now that she has left The Awful behind.

Adrienne cannot do chemo day on her own (nor does she want to) and the next couple of days it's necessary to be watchful, so she needs me both physically and emotionally from Tuesday through Friday morning. During that time I massage the body parts that are presenting neuropathy symptoms to increase circulation, act as a sounding board about whether or not she should take this medication or that, lift her up if she needs it, and generally mother her by taking care of chores so she can rest.

Adrienne loves so much being on her own in her space, so I am very grateful and lucky that I can head up to Barrie to spend time with my family there on the weekends. Scott and Stephanie have set up a lovely space in their house where visitors can stay that includes a dresser and a place to hang my clothes so I don't have to live out of a suitcase. There is nothing like coming up the stairs and seeing those little faces smile a "Good morning, Grandmaman". Or having one of them run up to get a kiss for a bobo. Or coming up with a book and looking at me saying "Uppa" (translation "hey Grandmaman, can I sit on your lap while you read this to me?") Isabelle pops over when her busy schedule allows or runs out of her house to give me a hug as I walk by on the way back from the park. It's just...lovely.

During The Awful Adrienne needed me almost all of the time. When getting up hurts, when you have to make a constant effort not to throw up, when your body feels like it weighs a ton, you need someone all the time. And I am so INCREDIBLY OVERJOYED that with this cycle of chemo it's not like that. My heart ached for her all the time during The Awful, wishing so badly that I could take it away, and seeing her now chow down on some ribs and corn on the cob makes me want to do a naked happy dance down the street.

There this one thing, though. Even though she doesn't need me all the time, I can't go home. And the honest truth is that there are some days I really want to go home.

I can't go home because I live a country away and if the shit hit the fan on a Saturday, like her feet hurt so much she needed to take the big girl pain meds and she shouldn't be alone, or if she got some kind of an infection and had to go to the hospital, I need to be close enough to get to her quickly. She needs time to have a break from her reality while she can, and I'm glad to give it to her, but if I lived closer, I could be going back and forth from her world to mine. When she was okay to be alone, I could be in *my* own space, sleep in *my* own bed. I could grab my grandchildren and sneak them off for some ice cream. Or maybe even have Elliott for a sleepover. If I lived closer...

I know that what I am doing now is one of the most important things I have ever done. Nothing can or will change that. She is flesh of my flesh, bone of my bone, and I love her more (to infinity and beyond The End I win). I am still as full of gratitude as I have always been about all the support I have that allows me to be here. Yet understandably, I think, I have moments of weakness, when I am feeling overwhelmed by all of this, when I am missing home and what the memories of home represent. The time before, when my child didn't have cancer.

Where sometimes in my mind's eye I am sitting cross-legged in a meadow plucking a flower...

She needs me, she needs me not.

Hey Mr Pavlov Nice to Meet You

Tuesday is chemo day, and there's a pattern to it now that we've passed week five. It's a long-ass day...blood work, seeing the oncologist about the blood work and how she's feeling (Adrienne, not the oncologist...her oncologist is a he), waiting for the chemo cocktail to be created, chair time, home. Most of the time there is enough time between the oncologist and the treatment to head downstairs to the cafeteria for breakfast and an extra cup of coffee. There is a simple joy in being able to use the stairs to get from the first floor to the second, because during The Awful that was impossible. Small miracles...

The stairs are right off the oncology department and the exit is directly beside the cafeteria. This past Tuesday we used them on the way out after treatment was done and when I opened the door I experienced what can only be described as panic, the fight or flight response like I had opened the door and there was a six foot rabid squirrel standing there, fangs bared, ready to launch an attack. And what generated this response, you might ask?

Smells.

WTF?

During The Awful, smells were one of the enemies. With the nausea ever-present, turning a corner and smelling anything could stop Adrienne in her tracks. She traveled with a mask that could filter the smells out or would put the end of her scarf over her face if she didn't have time to get the mask on. I became hyper-aware of smells so if by chance I sensed it first I could warn her to cover up, often walking a little bit ahead of her and sniffing the air. Mother Bear protecting her cub.

But it's been at least five weeks since smells were a problem, and now Adrienne can genuinely take pleasure in the scents of the world around her and can manage the nasty odors without worry. So once again, WTF Debbie? And then I made the connection.

Supporting my child through chemotherapy has created a conditioned emotional response in me to strong smells. It doesn't happen all the time, but when it does it isn't pretty. And once I made the connection to that one response, I realized there are others.

I have a conditioned response to salad. During The Awful one of the few things that was tolerable to Adrienne was a cool crisp salad, so we ate a lot of them. The thought of eating a salad right now turns my stomach a little bit.

Adrienne ate a LOT of watermelon. Unfortunately, I now have a conditioned response to that, too. One of my favourite things in the whole world. The thing I ate as my wedding supper because it was the only thing that appealed to me. When I think of eating it now it's a weird sort of sensation. Not the same as salad. The only way I can describe it is that it's like I see watermelon in black and white instead of colour. It has no appeal at all.

Pudding was the thing that allowed Adrienne to take the CBD oil that helped boost her appetite. Vanilla is my preferred flavour, with lemon meringue a close second. If I were asked in a survey now about my emotional relationship to pudding if it were a person my response would be B.) I would choose to spend time with pudding over many other foods. Yeah, pudding is in my important relationships category these days.

Hey Mr. Pavlov, nice to meet you.

Footnote: If that name doesn't ring a bell (you'll love that I said that if you know who Pavlov is) it's worth a Google or two.

.

Tuesday Leave 'Em Hotdogs, Wednesday Rage Pancakes, and Sunday Drives

Previously, on My Daughter's Boobs Are Trying to Kill Her...

Where sometimes in my mind's eye I am sitting cross-legged in a meadow plucking a flower...She needs me, she needs me not.

Well let me tell ya...

On chemo day to minimize the risk of allergic reaction to the Taxol, they give Adrienne a BIG dose of steroids before they hook up the chemo. The nurses have warned us that the steroids tend to cause one of two things...ravenous appetites or rages.

We got home on chemo day last week and we were both tired, since the day started earlier than usual, and they were running late. Sleep is a nonstarter for her on a good day and I, well, I'm her Mom and she's going in for chemo the next morning so Monday sleeps suck for me, too. I was trying to think of what we could easily eat from what was in the house and suggested hotdogs and oven fries and salad. (Yes, we're back to eating salad. But only certain kinds are allowed past the threshold. The others are held back by various relics hanging above the door). And you might be cringing at hot dogs but healthy food on chemo day? Ain't nobody got time for that!) Adrienne's in, so we get home and unpack our stuff and start cooking. Adrienne likes her hotdogs fried and I like mine boiled so there were two cooking styles going. She was managing the stove part while I was making salad and then SQUIRREL. She just walked away. From the stove. With a frying pan on high cooking hotdogs. I waited for a minute or two to see if she would come back but nope, so I calmly stepped in and finished cooking them for her. She ate three hotdogs, an entire bag of chopped salad, a serving of fries and topped it off with two pieces of apple pie. Ravenous, indeed.

And a petal falls...

On Wednesday morning I was having a bit of a lie in, which is an old-fashioned way of saying I was too lazy to get up right away when I woke up, so I just rolled over and looked out the window. All of a sudden, I hear a lot of banging and clanging and chopping and cursing in the kitchen and think oh oh, what's up? So, I roll out of bed, walk to the kitchen door and say "Good morning, daughter" and it starts. Raging at this (violently scooping pancake batter out of the bowl fiercely dumping into the frying pan), ranting at that (flipping the pancake and smashing it down with the spatula) eyes bugging out of her head (throwing used utensils into the sink).

"Adrienne how about maybe doing some leg lifts or something to help physically manage this?"

INCENSED AT THE WORLD SEETHING (because she is half French she talks with her hands and the spatula she is holding is crazily waving around as she simultaneously does squats and spews venom while watching pancake batter bubble).

She serves up the pancakes and we stand at the counter together eating them and she says...

"I guess Wednesdays will be Rage Pancake Day, huh Mom. Do you think these are a little salty?"

Another petal falls...

We both drove up to Barrie this past Thursday because Adrienne needed a kid fix and to talk some financial stuff with my son in law, and she thought it would be good for her to just get out of the house for a while. She had plans for the weekend with friends in the city but doesn't like to drive much anymore so it was decided she would take the train back to Toronto and I would drive her car back on Monday night. On Sunday, the little ones were on my phone video chatting to Grandpapa when the phone rang (like, a real phone call) and it was Adrienne.

"Mom, I have a fever and it's been going up all afternoon."

When we went to chemo teaching the one thing they emphasized multiple times was, if you have a fever, go to emergency. You get a little red card that tells them you're a chemo patient so they can treat you more quickly because with your immune system shot, time is of the essence if you have an infection. I've never driven so fast to Toronto in my life. I took her to emergency, they did blood work and x-rays and urine tests and IV fluids and IV antibiotics and after six hours, thankfully, we got to go home. The fever came down and the results were okay so it was "We're thinking virus so tuck yourself into bed and take extra care, young lady".

Another petal falls...

Okay universe...message received.

Where sometimes in my mind's eye I am sitting cross-legged in a meadow plucking a flower...She needs me, she needs me not. And the last petal to fall is always going to be, she needs me.

Rocks, Sand, Water and a Jar

There's an often used visual out there where professors place rocks into a jar until it appears to be full, then the professor shows you the jar is not really full by adding fine grains of sand. The grains of sand slip and slide their way through cracks until they settle somewhere inside. Once again, the jar appears to be full. And then the professor adds water, which slips in between the rocks and grains of sand. So, when something appears to be full, there can actually still be more room.

I recently sent my big brother what I thought was a funny picture of Adrienne during chemo, wearing big headphones and a koala sleep mask. He messaged me back that he was glad I could find some humour in it. I messaged back that I am numb to the horror of it. I have to be. This is my child in that chair. And watching her go through chemo every week is a big rock. After being paralyzed by despair the first time they hooked her up I knew I couldn't do it every week unless I built up some protection. So now when the big rocks hit I'm wearing a protective vest so I only feel part of the pain as each one slams into me. That allows me to pull up my big girl socks and march on.

Recently I've come to realize, though, that it's not the big rocks that are my worst enemy.

The grains of sand slip past my protective vest, rubbing between it and my skin until they break through. The grains of sand are those little "by the way" moments when we meet with the oncologist. Like nerve pain that will never go away. Like can't do anything about nails lifting. Or eyebrows and eyelashes hanging on during The Awful only to be taken by this cycle, the "easier" one. Sometimes I don't even notice the grains of sand are there until I start to bleed. That's when I feel on the verge of tears for no immediate reason. When I feel like I can't get enough air. When my ears ring. When I want to curl up in the fetal position and cover my head with a blanket. I can't do that, of course. Most of the time if it's during the day I'll go for a walk until it subsides. Put on my headphones and listen to an audiobook as my body finds a rhythm of breathing again. The worst is when it happens at night, because that means tossing and turning and a sleep filled with helplessness dreams or needing to get away but only being able to move in slow motion.

But even the grains of sand are not my worst enemy. My worst enemy is the water.

We were all overjoyed when the BRCA gene test came back negative, because we understood that to mean that once the treatment was successfully over, Adrienne would be able to have her body back. A few scars, yes, but the book of her cancer story would be mostly closed, with the possibility of a return to new kind of normal in her future. But this week's "by the way" moment with the oncologist was bigger than a rock, was sharper than a grain of sand. This week's "by the way" moment was a tsunami.

Because her cancer is Estrogen Receptor Positive, the best way to stop it from recurring is to suppress her ovaries, because they are the estrogen factory. They can do it chemically until she is finished with childbearing, take her off the medication so she can have her baby and then put her back on it. But the best way to suppress her ovaries is to take them out.

To take...them...out. She's 28 years old. And she knows now that her body will be in this fight forever. So much for closing the book.

So now I sit, crossing my fingers that some of the water that just filled up my jar will evaporate before anything else gets dropped in there. Because right now, it's pretty full. It's dangerously full. And my daughter needs me not to drown. Thankfully as of now there's a little room in there.

But eventually...

Shared Misery, Shared Hope

From the beginning, one of Adrienne's greatest concerns has been that she would disappear, that the cancer would end up being all she was about to the world, that it would own her. In private, just like most people, she's good to hang out in her sweats and a big sweater and play video games on the couch. She allows herself to be tired, to be angry, to wish. But she is very careful about how she presents herself to the public. Every outfit, every head covering, every piece of jewelry, every stroke of the eyebrow pencil is calculated so that when she looks in the mirror on her way out, she sees Adrienne, not the cancer patient. And that's important because if that's who she sees, she can carry herself with confidence regardless of the obvious impact the chemo has had. As a result, one of the most common greetings she gets from people who know but haven't seen her is "You look SO good". That's what anyone would like to hear but for her it's an extra boost, and it's also an "Oh Snap" moment when she knows she doesn't meet any of their preconceived notions of how cancer will have changed her appearance. While she does look amazing, especially considering all she's going through, I think a lot of what they're also sensing is also her spirit. She is not projecting "my life sucks feel sorry for me". She is projecting "I'm kickin' ass and taking no prisoners".

A couple of weeks ago I had to rush back from a visit with the family in Barrie to take Adrienne to emergency because of a fever. Fever can equal infection which in a cancer patient undergoing chemo can quickly develop into something life threatening. While we were in the registration area, a young woman wearing a mask approached us with a few questions. She was in emergency because she had recently had mastectomy after a diagnosis of Stage 3 breast cancer and she had a complication called lymphedema, a collection of fluid caused by lymph node removal that creates swelling in the arm. Adrienne really wasn't feeling well so we couldn't stay long but we answered what we could and I gave the young woman a hug as we left and told her she could do it.

Today was chemo day, and Adrienne was in the chair hooked up when that same young woman walked by. She looked at us and stopped. I'm paraphrasing, but this is how it went.

"Oh my goodness I can't believe it. Ever since I saw you in the hospital I've been thinking about you. From the news of my cancer I was very down and when I saw you in the hospital I was really low because of having the swelling, and being afraid of chemo and losing my hair. Then I saw you and you're so young and even though you were sick you were still carrying yourself so well, and I thought, that's how I'm going to do it. I'm going to face cancer like that. Thank you so much. You were an inspiration to me."

I sat there, listening. Looked at Adrienne's face. Saw and heard the reactions of the staff and other patients. Looked again at Adrienne's face. And as I had before, I got up and hugged the young woman, hoping that the inspiration would be enough.

Then, like any two young women, they had a quick talk about where Adrienne got her hat. Apparently, that was one of the things that had impressed her when she first saw us. How cool Adrienne looked in her hat.

Today, shared misery got pushed behind a blooming, fragrant flower field of shared hope. And for a moment, it made everything just a little bit sweeter in that awful room, a place where people really need as much sweet hope as they can get. Serendipity...

Seven Percent

Remember my jar?

There was more talk today with the oncologist about ovarian suppression post radiation and what the options might be. This discussion was more about the drugs that can be used and potential benefits and side effects which are a pretty big deal when you're going to be on the medications for five years.

Right now, the chemo induced menopause symptoms are making Adrienne so uncomfortable (she said using a milder description when it should say making her feel FUCKING TERRIBLE). Hot flashes, night sweats, those lovely sleep cycles where you can't get to sleep and then when you do you can't stay asleep, weight shifting to her belly. And that's on top of all the other stuff...UGH.

There are sort of three levels of ovarian suppression treatment. Removing the ovaries is Level one. Level three is Tamoxifen which attaches to the hormone receptors in the cancer cell, blocking estrogen from attaching to the receptors. This slows or stops the growth of the tumor by preventing the cancer cells from getting the hormones they need to grow. Level two is chemically induced ovarian suppression, which the oncologist acknowledged had lots of side effects like "roaring hot flashes". It's an important discussion to have, he says, because...

"Studies show that there is a seven percent less chance of recurrence with Level two, and that means that by using that option I save seven lives".

My heart stopped. The oncologist, this man that I trust is doing all he can for my child, was very clearly excited about that seven percent.

I am cognitively aware that the treatment Adrienne is undergoing has the goal of keeping her alive, but it's not something I can think about. Because if I think about this saving her life, I have to acknowledge it might not. And that is unthinkable.

Glug...glug...glug

The Shoe Dropped

It's been eleven weeks of treatment with Taxol. Only one more treatment to go. And the goddam shoe dropped. Guard is down. Looking at the home stretch thinking…

"Yeah she's gonna make it".

Silly me.

The discussion at the beginning of this treatment included talk of how the side effects usually kick in around the halfway point (week six) and in Adrienne's case, if she could hang in there, the oncologist wanted to push through because his end goal is to cure her. So, there was much excitement as week six, then seven, then eight went by and it seemed like she'd catch a break in this and cruise through. There was some tingling, some pain in her feet and hands, but it was manageable.

Then this week. I want to scream. I want to punch walls. I want to break dishes. I so desperately wanted this not to happen.

Her hands are not working properly. She says it feels like they are less sensitive and more sensitive at the same time. She opens and closes them often, an unconscious action I think, as her body tries to figure this out. She needs her hands and fingers to function so she can put on her public face, which she says is taking longer and longer each day. She is still trying to work, but it's computer work and guess what folks...she needs her hands and fingers to function to do that, as well.

Her feet are the same, with the added glory of numb toes. She can walk a little bit but then it starts to hurt...a lot...so one thing that she was really enjoying, going for walks in the afternoon, is no longer an option that she won't have to pay for. Oh, and walks make her hands worse, too. WTF.

Last night her back hurt so much she was wincing. We tried multiple things to make it feel better, both medication and heat, which touched it but didn't ease it very much. I sat beside her as she breathed deeply in preparation for the pain as she shifted forward on the couch to stand up. My heart breaking, yet again, because my baby is hurting and there is nothing I can do to make it better.

My emotions during all of this have ranged far and wide, but right now I am SO angry at this disease. Cancer is relentless, and as a result cancer treatment has to be tougher, smarter, sneakier. There are so many tradeoffs, and way too many of them are, in a word, terrible.

Oh yeah, then there was the latest BTW moment in the oncologist's office.

"Unfortunately sometimes Taxol side effects happen weeks after the treatment is over. There's just no way to tell how your body will react".

So the shoe dropped. Into my jar. The universe can be a very cruel place.

Today Has Been a Very Weird Day

Today was the last of twenty chemotherapy sessions. You'd think I'd be overjoyed right? You'd think I would want to shout from the highest mountains, take out a full-page ad in the New York Times, stop everyone I see to tell them the good news.

I did have a moment there, in the room when I saw that the last bag was empty, with the monumental realization that she'd made it. She toughed out all the side effects so they could push through to the end, maximizing her chances of the dragon being slayed. Twenty weeks of stress, of pain, of loss, of exhaustion. I couldn't be more proud of her. I wept, almost uncontrollably, for about ten minutes.

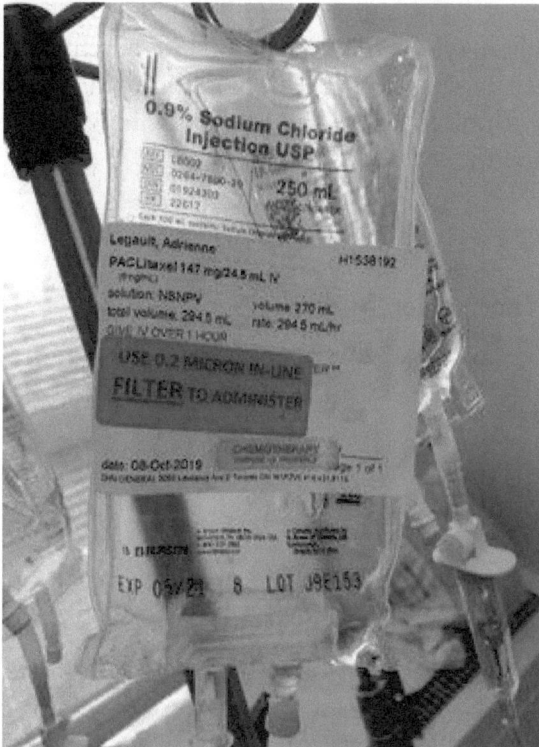

And then...nothing.

We rode home for the most part in complete silence. When we came in the house, she went into her room to hide for a while and sleep off the Benadryl as she often tries to do. I did the dishes and some laundry and organized a few things that have been lingering with the busy life we've led around here lately.

And still...nothing.

I know it's there, It has to be, right? I feel a bit nuts, to tell you the truth, because how I'm actually feeling versus how I anticipated I would feel have no commonality at all. The one thing I can clearly identify I'm experiencing is the sense that I am slogging my body through mud. My arms and legs feel weighed down. I'm humming with fatigue. The scientist in me says that maybe I've been running on adrenalin and with chemo over it's shut down. But there's more to come, so I really don't think that's it. But you know how I feel about the not knowing?

Nothing.

Today has been a very weird day.

The Little Things

Forty-eight hours have passed since that last bag of chemo finished dripping. As I said earlier, I expected it to be a big deal and it was more like a "whatever" moment emotionally. As a team Adrienne and I have been going through this process since May 29th. That's a short time in the grand scheme of things but it's forever when your child is going through it. I am still a bit "huh" about it being so anticlimactic, but I think I've figured it out.

In between Stephanie and Adrienne, I had three miscarriages. Of course, I grieved at the time, but the thing I remember the most was being on a camping trip with friends in Yugoslavia shortly after the second one and saying yes to the offer of a glass of wine. As I reached for it my hand froze in mid air because I realized that the only reason I could say yes was because I had lost a baby. I stared at that glass of wine for a good ten minutes before I took a sip, and as I did my eyes filled with tears. Like one more time saying goodbye to the dream.

So I think it's going to be the little realizations that move us forward, the things that got put in the "not really worth worrying about" category in the moment because there were so many things that were heavier to carry. Collectively they are monumental, and in that sense I am glad that those moments will come here and there, over the course of time, so that each can be adjusted to before another comes into play. Here's an example.

Yesterday I told Adrienne that I have an appointment for a pedicure and she got this odd look on her face and asked me to repeat the date. When I told her she looked at me and said...

"Hey, I can also get a pedicure on October 26th".

Puppy dog head tilt.

A little thing, but really a big thing, because of what it actually means. Her immune system will be recovered enough not to worry about an infection. Adjustment one.

It's recommended that while undergoing Taxol chemo that patients don't drink alcohol because it can increase the severity of the side effects. When it's your hands and feet not functioning properly you really don't want to do anything to make it worse than it is because it's pretty bad to begin with. Several weeks ago, we bought a fifth of Glen Livet with the plan to crack it as soon as enough of the chemo has left her system so it won't cause her any harm. Someone else said they'd come join us and "You're not allowed" shot out of my mouth before I could do anything to reign it in.

I expect that I will look at that glass of scotch in my hand for a few minutes, clink glasses with her, and watch her bring it to her lips. I expect it will take my breath away. I expect my eyes will fill with tears. Because it's one more step that means I get to keep my baby.

The little things...

The Awful, a Reflection

Adrienne and I had an interesting conversation last night about the process thus far and what is yet to come. Part of that was, and I know this sounds crazy, ranking the different treatments she has gone through since the diagnosis in March from worst to...can't say best because no no no, so...least worst.

The Awful has its own category because it was so much worse than anything else.

Adrienne and I still haven't talked about it much. I know it still makes me want to curl up into the fetal position and weep when I think about it, so I cannot imagine what it must be like for her. As I am sitting here typing this, I am a hair's breath away from tears. My ears are ringing a little bit, my stomach is rolling over, and my hands are starting to sweat.

Chemotherapy is a very cruel thing. It has to be to slay the dragon. I've written about the side effects that were expected and unexpected. How Adrienne managed them and what it felt like to help her do that. In our conversation last night, we agreed that the little things after The Awful ended were all about food. Food and smells.

There were some favourite foods that she couldn't stomach during The Awful, either because of the taste or because of the smell of it cooking. After it was done, she slowly but surely would eat and enjoy them and those were such secret fireworks and cheerleaders moments for me. She knew she had to eat during The Awful, especially knew her iron needed to be kept up, so she would eat small pieces of steak along with the cucumber and watermelon. She still can't eat steak and doesn't know if she ever will.

"I choked it down because I knew I needed iron to make sure I could continue treatment, but it was very hard".

My face didn't show it but that punched me in the gut. She was constantly on the verge of vomiting and she still choked down steak. What a fucking powerhouse she is.

But you know what the most cruel part of The Awful was?

That in between treatments, she would feel better.

The Awful was once every two weeks. The first week became relatively predicable, with the side effects becoming increasingly worse because of the cumulative nature of the chemo. By the end the side effects extended into the second week but there were always a few days when she felt better. Not good, but better. I'm having difficulty putting how I feel about that and what it meant into words. But what I've come up with is this.

Imagine that you're told in order to live, once every two weeks for eight weeks they have to break one of your fingers. The first time you don't know what it will feel like but hell yeah, if that's what it takes to live you go for it. It hurts, a lot, but it's not as bad as the alternative so you put on your big girl pants and suck it up. And then just as it starts to feel better, you have to break another one. But this time, you know exactly how that will feel. And you have to sit there and let them do it. They're kind, they're as gentle as they can be, and you keep your game face on. You've numbed up the area so it won't hurt when they actually do it, but you know that in a few hours you'll feel all of it. And that happens again. And again.

I'm thinking maybe some of you will now have rolling stomachs and sweaty hands thinking about what you just read. That isn't my intent. My intent is for you to understand just how much courage people going through chemotherapy actually have.

So much courage...

Schrodinger's Cancer

It's been eighteen days since the last dose of chemotherapy. Eighteen days of reflecting on why how I'm feeling isn't how I expected to feel. Eighteen days of still being watchful. Eighteen days of trying to adjust, little thing by little thing, to being free. Eighteen days of accepting that while some things are better, some are worse, because the buffering effect of some of the drugs have worn off, but thankfully it's more than likely that pain will ease up with time. Eighteen days that included an amazing visit and adventures with my brother and his wife, which was a more joyous and welcome distraction than I think they will ever know. Eighteen days of realizing a chapter is closed, but at the same time coming to terms with the fact that there is still a way to go before the climactic scene. And therein lies the rub.

November 20th. Surgery day. Lymph nodes dissected and sent for analysis. Then the unbearable-and-soul-crushing-unless-you've-been-there-you-can't-know anxiety waiting to find out. Is it dead or alive? Was it worth what she went through over the last eight months? Does she get her life back?

I just want her to get her life back.

I want her to go dancing. I want her to be able to drive on a freeway with the windows open and the wind lifting her hair...her own hair. I want to hear her sing. I want her to be able to wear her fancy shoes without worrying about her feet. I want her to go to Peru.

Any parents reading this will potentially think, "I want all of those things for my children, too. Except maybe Peru. That's just weird." And I give credit to you for that. At the same time, however, I'm going to play the cancer card.

Many of us have the thought "a piano could drop on my head and kill me tomorrow" lurking as we make life decisions sometimes (or a big snake in Peru...I would never want to go there) . Most of us at some point in time think about our mortality. I know that for me, though, thinking about my child's mortality is a very different thing. And I've had to think of it a lot lately. The fear, the helplessness, the hope. Feeling her spirit ebb and flow as her body recovers, knowing when she puts her head on my shoulder she's saying...

"Mommy I'm done. Can we go now?"

Feeling such love for her, such pride, such gratitude. Knowing the burden she's carrying, how heavy it is, and only being able to hold her up as she does it, because I can't really take any of it on. It's...a lot.

After eighteen days of reflection I've come to this. While I thought that after chemo finished the burden would be lighter, it is just as heavy, but in a different way. I think it's really not humanly possible to process all of the steps involved in fighting cancer at once. I think if you knew everything that was coming from the beginning, you might just give up before you started. So, you face things, one step at a time, one appointment at a time, one unknown at a time. Chemo is done. The next step is surgery to find out if it worked. And then the waiting to know. I hate the waiting. We are already planning a lot of things to fill up our days, believe me. We've been there before.
And for the duration of this particular wait, the cancer is both dead and alive. Hope makes it dead. Self preservation makes sure you acknowledge that it could be alive. There is no way to tell until someone lifts the lid off the box, until a

pathologist looks at the lymph nodes and makes a pronouncement.

Schrodinger's cancer.

The Little Things Part Deux

There is a lot of information out there about the stages of grief. Denial, Anger, Bargaining, Depression, Acceptance. I think for most people these stages are associated with big losses, like the death of a loved one, probably because of the Kubler-Ross work that brought the idea into the public consciousness. My experience in the last eight months watching my daughter manage cancer has, however, opened up a whole new world of grieving for me, a world of minutiae when reflected in the mirror of Adrienne's cancer diagnosis. It took me a while to make the connection, but I am thankful for having been both educated about and having experienced grief because it has made it much easier for me to understand when Adrienne's behaviour seems a bit odd, even for her in her current reality.

I was ready for the big ones. Like going bald, like not being able to work, like not being able to drive, like losing her independence. I was also prepared to be the target of her anger because my presence was a living breathing representation of why the losses were happening, and it's always easier to lash out at what's in front of you.

There were days when I would feel the anxiety and anger and see her working to manage it and always look at my own behaviour to see if I was doing anything that could be bothering her. I would see her hide in her room for a couple of days, and I would think of ways I could get out of her space hoping that would help. I would hear my mother's voice in my head saying "What can I buy you to make you feel better?" because I was grasping at straws. Because it's been a while since she went bald, since she couldn't work, since she couldn't drive, since she lost her independence, so this must mean she was simply being overwhelmed with the big things, all of them together, right?

Nope.

She was also ready for the big things. It's the little things, and the unexpected intensity of the grief at the loss of those things, that dumped us into the tank.

A blindingly bright wondrous thing happened during The Awful. She lost her hair...everywhere...except on her face. When we were out and about during The Awful at least ninety percent of the time people thought she had gone bald by choice because in no way did she look like a cancer patient otherwise. There were even a few fist-bump type reactions at the perceived activism of her "decision". She would walk away from those encounters grinning from ear to ear. Oh snap, Universe.

Unbeknownst to me, if Adrienne's hair has always been a thing of pride, her eyebrows have run a close second. While I always thought she created the look with products, it was always just her eyebrows all along. They arch perfectly, frame her eyes, add a touch of glamour to her face (if I sound biased, I'm allowed. I'm her Mom). And since The Awful hadn't taken them, she'd get to keep them, right?

Nope.

And never was the distinct pattern of the grief cycle more textbook than when she was losing her eyebrows. It took me a while to catch on, though. So many of what I perceived as worse things had happened, had been grieved, had been accepted. I was looking for obvious moments that I could "AHA" about, but this one was a lot more subtle.

First it was a couple of patches. She could easily fill those in with an eyebrow pencil, following the lines she still had. Not even talking about it, filling in the spots like it wasn't a problem. Denial.

Then it was only small patches of hair left, that when she took her makeup off at night increasingly ended up on the cloth.

"I'm so pissed off Mom. It took me a half hour to put on my fucking eyebrows this morning".

Anger.

She skipped Bargaining. There was nothing to offer up. What can you promise the Universe if you get to keep your eyebrows? The Universe is going to look back at you and say "Look...I helped you find the lump, okay?"

But she did not skip the next step.

"Mom, for the first time during all of this I look like a cancer patient. I don't see me when I look in the mirror. I can't go out in public looking like this. I don't even want the rest of the family to see me. I don't want to see the looks on their faces. I hate this. I'm going to take the time to put on my face before I come out of my room".

Depression.

That weekend we took a trip up to see the family in Barrie. She walked up the stairs at her sister's house, no makeup on, because she realized this is her family, who love her, who will see *her*, not the cancer patient. She's sitting on the couch playing with Clara when the Mommy says...

"Time to go to the park, Clara".

Clara stops at the top of the stairs, looking back and babbling at Adrienne.
"It's okay Clara, go see Mommy she'll put on your shoes".

Clara once again looks back and babbles at Adrienne, reaching out her arm.

"Do you want Auntie A to come to the park with you, Clara?".

Heh (Clara's version of yes). Adrienne gets up from the couch, picks up her niece, and walks down the stairs with her.

"Sure baby girl. Auntie A will come".

Out in public, no makeup on, lots of other adults at the park with their children.

Acceptance.

I will treasure that memory for the rest of my life. For the last step towards acceptance of a seemingly little thing, her eyebrows falling out, which for Adrienne was such a monumental loss, Adrienne was guided by another little thing, a little hand reaching out and pulling her heart strings across that bridge.

The little things...

Toilet Humor

Yesterday was a day. One of those ones that feel like the ground is shifting under my feet. A day that bounced between fighting tears and laughing really hard with my girl. One where her bubble and my bubble kept smashing into each other, me not knowing the reason why but feeling breathless and afraid. When I cross my fingers that sleep won't bring the helplessness dreams. Those are just the worst. And after a few tense moments of *that* kind of silence, followed by a long talk, we figured out why.

She is feeling better.

The body aches are gone. Some...not all but some...of the fog is starting to lift. She can drive again, not on the freeway yet but that's coming soon.. Her hair is starting to grow back (Mom I have FIVE eyebrow hairs!!). She's venturing out more, confident that she can get through a day without wilting partway through. The hot flashes are also easing, leading to great hope that her body will kick back into gear so carrying a child is in her future. Her face no longer looks like a full moon thanks to the steroids fully exiting her system, her body looks thinner as the bloating disappears.

Yes, she is feeling better. And life most days is blissful as a result. But remember the broken finger analogy?

In a few weeks, she goes in for more surgery. They are going in to take out the lymph node that tested positive back in May plus a bunch of its neighbours. And she knows just how bad that surgery is going to feel, how difficult the recovery will be, because she had a much smaller version of it in March when they did the sentinel lymph node biopsy. So much of the independence she has gained back, and as previously mentioned she is fiercely independent, is going to cruelly be ripped to shreds. She won't be able to pull up her own pants. She won't be able wash her whole body in the shower. She won't be able to stir cake batter. She won't be able to drive. She won't be able to type, or play video games, or wrap the beautiful scarves around her head. The potential long term side effects of this surgery, nerve damage, restricted movement and lymphedema, are devastating in particular because the armpit they will be cutting into is the left one, which is her dominant hand.

And she is not ready, acknowledges she will never be ready. She can do as much preparation as possible about the practical things, but that's about it. Oh my friends, there is such dread.

So what on earth did we laugh about yesterday?

After the first surgery one of the biggest complaints was a common side effect of pain medication, constipation. It got to the point that she was ready to go to emergency to get some help when things finally started to happen. This time around, she has medication she was given during chemo when she was prescribed drugs for the pain that will prevent that from happening, and she knows it works because she has already used it and it worked, um, a little bit too well truth be told. We're talking about that part of it yesterday and she looks at me and says with a sharp tone...

"Well at least that part of my life won't be in the toilet."

We were in the middle of a very serious conversation and I was so hoping she had noticed what she'd just done because I didn't know if I could hold it in. We made eye contact and burst out laughing, deep hearty laughter that came up from our toes. And because it was totally unintentional it made it even more funny to both of us. It lifted the moment and let us move forward with our day.

We are both grown ass women, we seriously are, but I guess toilet humour never gets old, right?

And I'm so glad it doesn't.

The Little Things Part Trois

This last month has been such an odd one. There have been some lingering symptoms of the Taxol, in particular muscle aches which have at times taken me back to when things were really rough, but her hands and feet have mostly recovered. I can see the five o'clock shadow on her head, in her eyebrows, and it's dark hair....HER hair. There are tiny little eyelashes growing back. Not enough to put mascara on, but they're coming. Every day brings another bit of normal back into life, another step away from all the horror and loss that came with the chemo. There are more and more moments of joy. They used to be so rare, but now they come daily.

And more often than not, when they come, it makes me want to cry.

They say cancer changes people, and I know that for the most part that is intended to apply to the person who has been diagnosed and goes through the treatment on the way to the other side. I think there needs to be another category, though, because cancer has also changed me. A lot.

If you know me other than this blog, you might have heard me talk about the fact that I "see" my life. I am not oblivious to the good fortune I have had, the risks I have taken that have turned out so well for me, the things that have gone my way when they really shouldn't have. I try my best not to take any of that for granted, because I know it could have gone very differently. The experience of supporting my child through cancer has changed that awareness, has taken it from dial up to broadband, where everything seems to come at me faster, from everywhere, and I see so much good that I used to miss. So many kindnesses. It's just...a lot.

When you're down, when life has given you a kick in the head, people's kindness means something completely different. It's like a point of light at the end of a dark tunnel, and when you've been in the darkness even a little bit of light shines so much brighter. It's not even people necessarily going out of their way, or thinking they are, that touch me that way.

Once again, it's the little things. Like getting my bangs cut for free. I drove away from that five minutes in the chair and started to weep. It wasn't a big deal for her, and I'm sure the number of times I thanked her seem a bit too many, but she has no idea what that meant to me. She didn't have to fit me in. She did it as a kindness. I had gone to two people prior to her and they had screwed them up royally. She fixed them. And now I am in good shape, hair wise, to go into the next six weeks during which time I'll be trying my best to help my child avoid losing part of the use of her left arm after surgery, so I can't be worrying having wonky bangs. Like I would, really, but I am trying to bring normal back to me, too, and wonky bangs...ain't nobody got time for that.

I am not sure I have the capacity to keep feeling this way, to have so much gratitude all the time. But I hope I do, because it's an amazing way to go through life, seeing all that I'm seeing now. A friend who has been fighting cancer for over a year told me at the beginning that I would experience something like this, and I thought she was nuts.

I don't think so anymore.

My Daughter Has Cancer

In August, when Adrienne was feeling so much better and I was driving both of us crazy by being in the house all the time, we both decided a good thing for me to do was get a job. One of those part time flexible jobs where you clock in, do your job, clock out, go home. Something to give me a chance to talk to other people, to have a routine based on something other than Tuesday being chemo day. So, I got a job...as a Costco Demonstrator. And man am I good at it! For example, a recent shift my job was to promote a laundry detergent called "Springtime". I got people to come in for the spiel by asking them if they would like a whiff of springtime on this cold winter day (-8 in November...BRRR) and I sold a whole flat. *Licking finger placing on chest making water hissing sound* Oh yeah...I'm that good.

And nobody I worked with or for knew Adrienne had cancer. There was no need to tell them, until I had to stop working because of her surgery next week and chose to let them know why I was leaving. This was the first time I've told new people Adrienne has cancer for what seems like forever. And you know what?

I might as well have heard about her diagnosis yesterday. Because that's what it felt like telling them. My throat tightened, I felt the same shock-y symptoms I had when I told people in March. I've been in a kind of zone where it's an elephant in the room with a big pink blanket over it. Everyone knows, acknowledges, but doesn't talk about it. And in those moments somehow not talking about it makes it less real. Oh I know it's real, and my increasingly sleepless nights are indicative of my anxiety rising as the surgery and the wait for the results approaches, but it's a weird kind of lovely pretending.

And even though I've only been there a short time I saw the sorrow in my coworkers eyes, felt them reach out to hug me and tell me they'd pray for her, asking me to keep in touch about her going forward. Many of the mothers were especially kind, one saying it's one thing when it's your Mom but your child...that's something she can't imagine.

I'm welcome to come back anytime, just a simple phone call to let them know I am available to work again. I have nothing in common with these women other than six hours when we all brace ourselves for the onslaught of people hovering and pouncing on our sample trays. That, and motherhood. And our membership in the motherhood club made them create a support bubble for me when I told them what was once again devastating news...

My daughter has cancer. My twenty-eight-year-old daughter has cancer.

Oh my God...my twenty-eight-year-old daughter has cancer. See me tomorrow when I get the elephant's foot off of my chest.

Real Talk

Yesterday we decorated Adrienne's house for Christmas. It's one of her favourite times of year and since her arm will be out of use for a while, she decided she wanted her house looking like Christmas before surgery tomorrow. We had a lot of fun, some great laughs, a life changing storage space found (MOM YOU'RE A WITCH), some easy and good food.

And then out of the blue the fear came and sat on my shoulder, whispering in my ear...

"Is this all you're going to get?"

And it was there, on my pillow, stretching and yawning alongside me as I woke up this morning.

"Better savor these moments because this could be all you're going to get".

It can't be, right? She's been through so much to get to the other side, to beat the monster and go on to live her life. This can't be all I get.

But the horror of my life right now is, it could be. It could be. Just as there's a chance, a great chance, she'll beat it, there is also a chance, a minuscule chance, that she won't. And once in a while I try to imagine how I would survive that. Because, you know, I like to be prepared. And it's very scary because I can't picture me there, at least not as the person I am now.

She is my child. I carried her inside my body, felt her come to life, heard her first breath, her first cry, watched her take her first step, her first fall, her first pirouette, her first love. It's not the way of things that I should also watch her

108

lose her life, hear her take her last breath, long to see her dance once more as I sift through the memories of holding her in my arms on a cold November day full of joy and laughter as we put the star on top of the tree. I should not have to flip through the pages of our lives feeling her little lips at my breast, her little hand in mine, her tearful hug goodbye when she went to school, yelling at me "MOM DON'T MOVE THE NEEDLE". I shouldn't have to do those things...not yet. Oh please not yet.

So I will put on my big girl pants today, dry my tears, and hold her up in preparation for her surgery tomorrow. But just for a moment this morning I guess I needed to step into that dark place, to confront it full on, to look fear in the eye and say...

"Maybe, maybe yes this will be all I'll get. Now you've had your fifteen minutes of fame this week, fear. Go away. My daughter needs me"

I can't really say this out loud to anyone, because the likelihood is that they would try to reassure me that everything is going to be okay. And I know that the fear is ready to jump back on my shoulder and say...

"But will it be okay?"

And I'm just a little too fragile today to be sure I could send it away another time.

The Lump Part Deux

Two days post-surgery. I'll surely be writing more about this part of the experience in the weeks to come, but for right I'm just taking care of my girl, keeping her drugged and fed, not necessarily in that order. And thankfully my mind has been occupied by the action side of mothering, because guess what the surgeon found when he went in to take out the lymph nodes?

A lump. A tiny shriveled dead looking lump. A non-threatening looking lump. A completely unattached and removed lump. A lump that was stopped in its tracks by the chemo, which is why the choice had been made to start chemo versus delaying it by the six weeks of recovery time necessary if they had taken it out back in May. He may have told me lots of important things surrounding that, about how well she did, about how he had taken a bit longer to do the surgery because he took some action to save the nerves, particularly because it's her dominant arm. About how significant it would be for her to make sure she gets the arm above her head by day three to ensure she keeps scar tissue from forming that would limit her range of motion. But you know what I heard?

He found a lump.

Back in April, when Adrienne met with the radiation oncologist after her initial surgery, he ordered some scans and when they came back wasn't happy with how one of the lymph nodes in her armpit looked. He ordered a biopsy and it came back positive which is why this surgery was put into the treatment plan to begin with.

Stay with me because there is math coming your way.

Adrienne received her cancer diagnosis on March 15th. The biopsy used to make the determination was done at the beginning of March. The lumpectomy and sentinel lymph node biopsy were done on March 27th. In preparation for the surgery, a guide wire was placed into the tumour that morning using ultrasound. The ultrasound showed that the tumour had grown by eighteen percent since the biopsy was done at the beginning of March.

Eighteen percent. In three weeks.

Eighteen percent might not seem like a lot, but when we're talking about a tumour it's terrifying. We had been told it was an aggressive cancer, but that was a gut punch.

The lymph node biopsy ordered by the radiation oncologist was the result of scans done in mid-April. Chemo started on May 29th. That means that we're talking six weeks, give or take, between when he noted the suspicious area in April and when chemotherapy was introduced to kill it.

Six. Weeks. Six weeks of growing time. Six weeks of spreading time. With a very aggressive cancer. Typing that is making me want to vomit.

So to all of you out there who thought she should get a second opinion, that she shouldn't blindly follow the medical system's choices about her treatment plan (oh yeah, folks, like you need to deal with that when you've been told you have cancer), that they were being too aggressive considering it was still just a lump, that she was putting herself through misery when she could have done it an easier way, I have four words for you.

He found a lump.

I could never have imagined that this thought would ever cross my mind, let alone that I'd express it. But here goes. Thank you, The Awful. You likely saved my child's life. From the bottom of my heart and soul, thank you. I also have four words for you.

I forgive you now.

Small Spaces

I've spent a great deal of my life living in small spaces, and as a result I've gotten pretty good at managing what comes with that, like finding every possible inch of storage and making sure the common area always gets picked up and tidied. This is especially important if your common area doubles as the play area because, well, Lego hurts. Or if someone happens to be living in it. Like me right now.

This...is my bedroom. Where I have been sleeping for eight months. Or not sleeping. Whatever...

My brother John makes his bed every day. He says doing it puts his day on the right track, or something like that. I make my bed every day, too. Not because I want to, or because it puts my day on the right track, but because if I don't half the living room is taken up by my mattress. At home I have a king bed, a walk in closet, a dresser, a vanity and a bedside table. See that white thing right there, that amazing Ikea thing my daughter bought me? That's my closet, my dresser, and my vanity all wrapped up into

113

one. My bedside table is the space between the end of the couch and the wall. Those things are hidden during the day and get put on the couch beside my head at night.

I just burst out laughing. Because it's ridiculous, isn't it? That a woman of my advanced age, who has lived and stayed in all these amazing places, would be content with this. But you know what I am?

I am grateful that I have a relationship with my daughter, who cannot STAND clutter, for whom chaos in her home creates true anxiety, that allows me to invade her space without her wanting to kill me. I am grateful that technology for air mattresses has moved into the realm of spectacular. I am grateful for the geniuses at Ikea who somehow keep outdoing themselves in the category of awesomesauce design. I am grateful that I have settled into the fact that my colour palette for clothes is monotone because everything I have in that little closet goes with everything else in that little closet. I am grateful that I can be content with my space right now, because being here is beyond necessary for me.

I am grateful. Once again I am fucking grateful. Someone needs to give me a new word for this emotion. Grateful is getting seriously old.

Motherhood Part Deux

A friend of Jane's contacted Adrienne in the summer because Jane, a 33-year-old mother of one, was diagnosed with breast cancer and the friend thought Adrienne might be able to help Jane through the process. One of the things that Adrienne has clearly identified over the course of her affliction (our pet word for it) is that she really doesn't have a lot of peers who can relate to what her experience is so she was happy to offer support to someone who was young enough to go through some of the same types of challenges during treatment. One of those clubs you join you really don't want to be in, ya know?

They messaged back and forth, Adrienne offering suggestions for managing some of the side effects like the nausea, taking action with the hair loss, maximizing her use of the days when she felt better. Adrienne understands like only one who is going through it that when it comes right down to it you're really on your own, because each individual cancer patient's body is going to react as only that body can, the mind is going to deal with emotions as only that person's mind can. Your support system can be crappy or amazing, but you're the ultimate factor in how it goes.

"Holy shit Mom Jane died".

I've changed the name out of respect for the family, but it really doesn't make a difference, does it?

I was walking across the living room when she said it and I froze in place as the shock reaction came on...the chill, the ringing ears, feeling the blood drain out of my face. Wait no no no that can't be because she's you...she's your peer...no no no no NO.

"Mom I have so many questions but I don't know if it's fair for me to ask them right now because the friend is so upset".

I had a question that I badly needed answered, too. It was a totally selfish moment for me, and I'll own that. I feel ashamed that one of the first thoughts that went through my head was...was it the cancer or was it treatment related. Because if it was the treatment, then we're past that part so I can take a breath about my own child's mortality. And once I take that breath, I can feel all the sympathy in the world for Jane's family. I can feel their pain, their shock, cry at the thought of a little girl growing up without her Mom. But until I have that answer, my vision has dangerously narrowed to my child's face, my ability to feel compassion strangled by an all encompassing, mind numbing, paralyzing fear.

Normally the fear just sits on my shoulder, whispering in my ear, and I can tell it to hush and move on. Yesterday it was a fucking monster, gnashing its teeth, baring its claws, ready to tear me to pieces. So, I just stood there and said...

"I don't think it's unreasonable for you to ask if it was the cancer or treatment related."

I'm working on forgiving myself this morning for my reaction, for the relief I felt, for once again being overwhelmed with gratitude when Adrienne read aloud the response.

"It was treatment related."

I often say that I think people's values, what they believe to be true about themselves, is situational. Before I had children, I would have sworn up and down until Tuesday that I could never take another human life. Once I became a mother, a situational change, I realized I'd throw you under a

116

bus in a heartbeat if you were threatening my child. I can't throw cancer under the bus. I'm helpless against this threat, so I have to somehow manage to sweep it to the corner of the room because if I shared my space with it any more than that I'd lose my mind. And that's what I think happened yesterday. Cancer was right up in my face, screaming at me…

"I could kill her you know"

And I lost my mind. Just for a moment, I lost my mind, and nothing else mattered other than knowing the answer to my question. It doesn't justify my reaction, but in that context, I think I can live with myself for having had it.

Sweep…sweep…sweep

The Results Are In

I've been told that I'm a pretty good writer. I check for grammar and make sure I don't use the same word too many times in a paragraph. I try to create linkages throughout a story. But as I am sitting here my hands are hovering over the keys not quite knowing what to do.

Today's BTW moment at the oncologist's office was...

That her lymph nodes are cancer free. She's cancer free.

And I simply have no words to express anything about that. I'm sure there will be some coming, but for now...

The end.

Coming to Terms

It's funny how you can get life changing news and it doesn't actually change your life.

That's the only way I can describe what the last couple of days have been like. I keep waiting for it, a little bit less patiently as each hour passes, that unicorns-fireworks-clouds parting moment, but I'm thinking maybe it's just not going to happen anytime soon. And I think maybe I know why.

My innocence bubble has been burst, and once it has been, you can't go back to living inside of it.

Ever.

Don't get me wrong. I'm so thankful that the treatment was successful, more than I can possibly express. My child suffered through an incredible ordeal, and she has more than earned the victory. It has given her family and friends a new perspective on what's important, how precious time is, how you can't waste a single moment. I have been holding her a little longer when we hug, finding it difficult to let go as I feel her body relax into mine. I have told perfect strangers in line at the grocery store because there has been an irresistible need to say the news out loud. It's an amazing thing to wake up in the morning and be able to say "*My child* had *cancer*". It truly is.

What I am coming to terms with, what I believe is putting a damper on the fact that we got the best news possible this week, is that this will never be over.

Ever.

Because she was so young when she got the diagnosis Adrienne qualifies for a special screening program that will

119

have her going in for yearly scans to check for a recurrence of the cancer. If I live another twenty years it will mean that there will be twenty more times that I have to wait for results. Twenty more times that I will have to answer the phone prepared for the news (I was so unprepared the first time, and I can't allow that to happen again, because I'm afraid it would end me). Twenty more times I will not be able to stop the fear from whispering in my ear.

The life changing news was hearing that Adrienne had cancer. It has altered my perception of my world, opened a window to a place I didn't know existed, forced me to put a protective wall around my heart and mind that I will never be able to take down. It has changed my relationship with me in ways that are so profound I haven't done more than dip my toe into the water of my new reality because I don't have it in me to pull myself up out of the water if I do any more than that. So once again I think, if I am feeling this way, what must it be like for her?

I know that some of you are thinking that I'm being pessimistic, that I should be celebrating this development, but the fact is that this was a battle. It was a big one, an important one, and for all intents and purposes, it should change the course of the war. But that's the kicker...we are still at war.

This will never be over for Adrienne, either, and because she's going to need me to be at the end of the phone I will stay out of the deep end, because she needs me to not drown

Ever...

34,560 Minutes

You know how changes can happen and because they're happening gradually you don't really notice how drastic they are? Check this out...

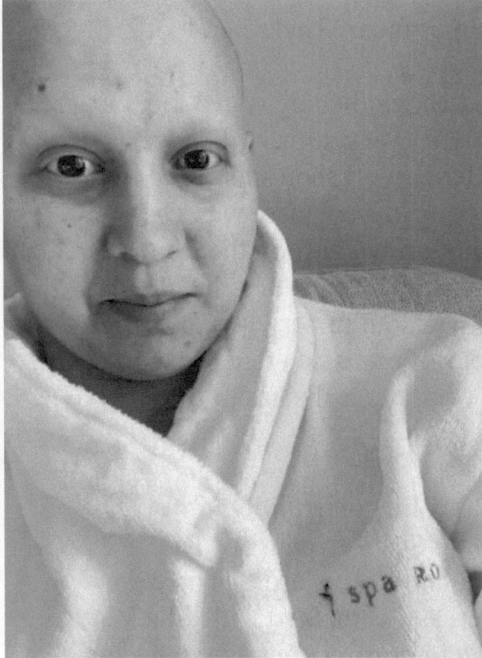

On the left is the face that Adrienne refused to show the world. The face that in her own words made her look like a cancer patient. The puffy steroid face. The one that thankfully she could disguise with artfully applied makeup when we needed to leave the house because she didn't want to experience the look-twice-don't-make-eye-contact stares from strangers as we passed by.

On the right is the face she has now. Remember those amazing eyebrows I wrote about? They're back. As are her eyelashes which now, in the words of one of our friends, cast a shadow. They are long enough to cast a shadow. The hair on her head is long enough that the cowlick is returning, the widows peak is back, and it's dark. Not grey, but dark. It's her hair, not some weird chemo hair.

And that little grin she has on her face? That's her, too.

One of the btw moments about chemotherapy is that there is no guarantee that what is lost will ever return. When we went to the Look Good Feel Better workshop sponsored by the Canadian Cancer Society back in May there was a woman there whose hair had not grown back in the front third of her head. Research, which you can't help but do, had many instances where it grew back but in wiry grey curls. A friend of Adrienne's at year four of remission told her that her eyebrows never came fully back and she has to fill them in all the time.

Can you imagine being 28 years old, going through treatment that you know is going to save your life, not knowing if you'll ever look the same afterwards? There are fears big and small with cancer, and compared with what could have been I know having to draw in your eyebrows for the rest of your life doesn't seem like a big deal. But you know what it would mean?

It would mean getting up every day, for the rest of your life, looking at your cancer patient face.

Of course there are scars from the surgeries that will remind her of this nightmare. There will be follow up scans and tests, drugs she'll have to take, decisions about when her ovaries come out. Flashbacks about The Awful that will drop her into a cold sweat. But she'll be able to face all of those things with her face, her before the cancer face, her perfectly arched eyebrows face.

And all she had to do was wait 34,560 minutes to see if that would be true. Do something for me here. Set a timer on your phone or watch a clock and see just how long one of those minutes is. Now imagine doing that 34,560 times.

I'd be grinning, too... 😊

At the Risk of Repeating Myself

I was about to type that this has been a very weird week, but then I thought do I have any so-called "normal" weeks anymore? I'm not even sure I'd recognize it if I did. That being said, I guess I'd have to propose that in my new life there are degrees of weird, and on that scale this one has been pretty close to a 10. I am back to not sleeping, back to waking up at four a.m. with my brain kicking in. It feels very much like it did back in the beginning when everything was new and unknown. I am having difficulty concentrating, half completing tasks. I put my phone into a laundry bucket full of little face cloths and such to take it downstairs with the towels to do a load of laundry at Stephanie's house and forgot I had put it there, dumped the bucket including my phone into the washing machine, and only realized what I had done when I went to listen to my audio book while I packed up my things. Thankfully it was on top and it's a bottom filling machine so I rescued it in the nick of time.

The appointment with the radiation oncologist was yesterday. It's the first time that I have met him, although I was on speaker phone in the room when he spoke to her back in the spring. The whole experience reminded me of what it felt like walking into the medical oncology clinic with Adrienne that very first time. I couldn't quite catch my breath. It felt like my limbs weighed a ton, my ears were ringing, I was fighting with all I have in me not to run. Once he was in the room and started to speak I had my arms and legs crossed in such a way that I couldn't have been protecting my vulnerable core any more without twisting myself into a pretzel.

This appointment was about how the radiation will proceed, the strategy behind the plan, what side effects she might encounter, how to mitigate them. It's six weeks of five days a week, and that takes us into mid February which is longer than we thought I'd have to be here. We both know that me being here when she doesn't need me isn't healthy for either of us, but I can't go home if she can't drive on the highway. Of all the the treatments she's undergone this one will be by far the easiest to manage, and once she's able to drive herself she's contemplating going on her own because that would mean she can send me home and start to reclaim her life.

But before all that starts, they're going to do a scan. And I'm afraid. I'm mind-numbingly afraid. The fear on my shoulder that normally just whispers in my ear once in a while is now my constant companion, invading my every waking moment, and unfortunately I'm awake a lot right now. I keep telling it to hush, that the tests say she's cancer free, that the monster is dead, that she's going to be fine.

And it whispers back...

"Not until he says so".

You see, this is the guy who found the second cancer, the one in her lymph nodes, that made the third surgery necessary. The one that made her once again the girl with cancer after we had been told by other members of her team that she was cancer free. When he spoke to us yesterday he was very positive about the treatment's success and the likelihood that any satellite growth has been wiped out the same as the one in her lymph node was. But he didn't say that she's cancer free yet. That's what the scans are for.

So at the risk of repeating myself, I'm sitting here once again waiting for the other shoe to drop. And silently screaming at the universe that I have enough goddam shoes.

Now where the heck is my phone...?

The Water, Part Deux

So...for the second time in nine months, I'm sick. I'm such a cliché.

I have been back and forth to visit the grandchildren multiple times, and we know little people are petri dishes of disease, especially once they're in school. I have ridden on buses, trains, been in and out of hospitals more times than I can count, even flown once. I worked at Costco for a couple of months handing out samples to hundreds of people, and although I wore gloves, I didn't wear a mask to stop their airborne germs from flying across the space between. But nothing. Zilch. Nada. So why now?

Looking back on it, both times I have been ill have been when Adrienne was in a golden time. That's where she is now, her recovery from the surgery going much better and faster than expected. These are the times when I can take a breath, slow down the velocity of my brain flashing here there and everywhere trying to ease her distress. Isabelle is also doing well; her job is continuing and her living arrangements are good. Stephanie and Scott have adjusted perfectly to her going back to work full time, as have the little ones. So in this moment no one that I am geographically close to needs me, not in the physical action mothering kind of way anyway.

It's amazing how the body carries on, defying the odds, when it has to. How it fights off germs, deals with little sleep, holds onto calories because the stress level is so high it thinks you must be in some kind of danger. And it's just as amazing how quickly it crashes, losing all the protection in what seems like one fell swoop.

You'd think the protective shield would have stayed up, considering the scan is still upcoming, but since I put that fear on the page for all to see it seems to have tucked itself into the corner with the swept-up cancer for the moment. I was pondering why now when I realized something that has also only happened twice since this all started occurred last week.

I got drunk and as a result I had a good cry.

I have fought the good fight over tears. I've pushed them back, felt my eyes well up and pinched myself both figuratively and literally to hold them at bay. A few of them have escaped through a hole in my defenses but I have quickly shored them up. I've had some very happy tears, like when the lymph nodes came back negative or when her eyebrows came back, or when I read Jacquie's news. But sad tears, not something I have let flow for long for fear they wouldn't stop. Plus I'm the Mom so...yeah.

Last week the dam burst. It was after the appointment with the radiation oncologist and I had been so anxious I cracked a beer as soon as we got back here. Then I cracked another one. And a third. Then I started to cry. Adrienne and I had a profound talk about her cancer, another thing that if I really think about it has also only happened twice since I've been here. We've spoken about side effects and practical things, but neither of us are built to share dives into the emotional part of what this has meant to her, and to me, and so we have, consciously I think, avoided going there.

Man, did we ever go there.

The dam burst, the tears flowed, and the water, which has always been my worst enemy, washed away my walls. And I got sick. For the second time in nine months. Of course I did.

But at least I've had a few days on the couch to rebuild...*sigh*...and I tell you Prime Suspect is a really good show.

The Cold War

The holidays have come and gone. Loved ones seen and held close, presents opened, food and drink, laughter and games shared a plenty. Late nights, early mornings with the pitter-patter of little feet and the "coffee, my kingdom for a coffee" look of desperation on the poor parents' faces. Grandparents getting to be solicitous and kind but getting to stay in bed just a little bit longer. At least for now. That will likely change in the future and it will be very welcome having little people come in for a morning snuggle.

And always, despite all the wonderful distractions, on the edge of my consciousness, a devastatingly clear understanding of just what a gift it was to look over and see Adrienne there.

Parent love is such an overwhelming force. I have watched her suffer physically and emotionally over the last year and it has broken my heart. I have rubbed her feet, her hands, her back, her head, anything to ease the pain. I have tried my best to stay out of her way when she needed me to. I have also celebrated many things with her, chemo endings, good test results, feeling hungry, hair coming back in...everywhere...the amazing Lululemon pants find. We have shared much, she and I, and only she and I will know what this whole thing was like.

It became very clear over the holidays that she's very much still struggling to process what she has been through, what she still has to go through, the decisions she still has to make that no 28 year old woman should have to make.

What also became clear over the holidays is that I have my own road to walk down as I contemplate my return to my own life, what this has done to me, how I am going to move forward. How I know that it's getting harder and harder to

129

contain the explosive anguish the last year's memories bring and I am pretty much walking around seemingly very aloof because it's the only way I can not break the seal. Because I just can't...not yet.

When Adrienne and I were in Japan we went to visit the Hiroshima Peace Memorial Museum. Patrons can choose to do a self-guided tour with headsets, and we thought it would be a good idea. At first, we were both a little overcome by the images and stories, and chose to separate so that we could each experience it in our own time and way, knowing that doing it together would somehow make it more difficult.

I think this is the same. I don't think either of us will be able to get to the end of this together. We will have to go our own ways, do it in our own time, and then join together after all is said and done and go for a coffee, maybe hold hands for a while. Like we did after the Peace Museum.

And I also think that unlike being able to close the book on the first experience, right now it will simply be ending a chapter. Although the biggest battle has been won, danger still sits on the horizon, and will for the rest of her life. A tenuous peace is in place, yes, but it's a wobbly bridge that insists you don't look down.

The Cold War begins.

Deer in the Headlights

One of the things I've had a lot of this last month is time, which for me means thinking. I've been off my game and trying to figure out why I was feeling so out of it. My first thoughts as I was leading into this episode of the story was sheep. How sheep supposedly blindly follow along, not really questioning why, moving forward along the path mindlessly, and that's sort of what my life has been recently. But that didn't feel right, not to describe what has been floating around my brain this last couple of days. A weird sort of sensation, like I'm here, but not here. This is happening, but not happening. And then it came to me.

I feel like a deer in the headlights.

My deer in the headlights moment was hearing the words "Mom, it's cancer" 296 days and 14 hours ago. And I'm pretty sure I've been in shock ever since.

The only analogy I can think of to provide a frame of reference is it's like being on a guided tour. There are so many people you encounter along the way who have so much more experience than you do with cancer. They're so calm and matter of fact about it. They have a sort of "been there, done that, bought the t-shirt" air about them because, well, they have. I can't fault them for any of it. It was all new to me, and I needed all the calm direction they could provide. So, I followed along, because this was Adrienne's hope, all of our hopes really, that she would win the war. That's why I first thought sheep, because it felt like that, constantly hearing this or that and saying "Okay, if that's what it takes, okay".

But I'm not a sheep. I'm a deer, caught in cancer's glare. The truth of the matter is that through all of those appointments, through all the days of misery and recovery, for every second of these last 296 days and 14 hours I have been silently screaming, at the top of my lungs, that this can't really be happening.

I can't be sitting here listening to them talk about nerve damage. I can't be holding my baby's hand while she cries out in pain during a procedure knowing it has to be done. I can't see her panic at smells. I can't hear her wince. I can't be changing dressings, and giving shots, and setting alarms in the middle of the night so her pain meds don't wear off. I can't be running for a bucket just in case.

My baby can't have cancer.

But she did. And I did do all of those things, and I'm beginning to think that I have been protected in part from all of this by still being in shock. And here's where things get tricky.

I have always been one of those people who is really good in a crisis, takes charge, gets things done, then falls to bits once it's dealt with, once the shock wears off, when it's safe for me to do so because it's over. But cancer is, as I've said more than once, never really over. No one can, unfortunately, unring that particular bell. So I can't really fall to bits, and with the exception of a few usually alcohol-fueled moments over the last year, I haven't cried. And now, I can't have those cathartic ugly crying moments that signify the end.

You may think I can but walk in my shoes and then lets talk.

So to those closest to me, if I act out of character in the coming months I'll ask your understanding in advance. This is new territory for me and I'm really at a loss as to how I'll navigate my way through. And to the universe, please hold off on sending anything else down the road right now.

You know, that whole deer in the headlights thing.

Mi Casa Es Su Casa...But Is It Though?

We got back from Radiation Day 3 this morning and as I was hanging up my things on the hooks by the door Adrienne said...

"This one is for the keys and this one is for your stuff".

I unthinkingly put my scarf on the key hook just for a second and OH MY GOD her head swung towards me like an Exorcist moment and this appeared on top of her head...

WHAT THE FUCK ARE YOU DOING MOM?!?!?

So as quickly as I could I picked up my scarf and moved it to the hook it was supposed to be on. Crisis averted.

Adrienne has been most welcoming, and I can't imagine what it's been like for her to have me parked in her living room for nine months give or take. There is no storage space, really, and so we have struggled to find places to put my suitcases and "stuff". She is very...particular...and I respect completely that it's her home and do my best to accommodate. One of the first things I said to her when I got here was that it was the little things that were going to cause us the most difficulty so it was important that she tell me as they came up so I could change what I was doing to avoid conflicts that were easily prevented. Her degree of...particularity...increases or decreases along with her anxiety, so as you can imagine there have been some days along the way when this would be me...

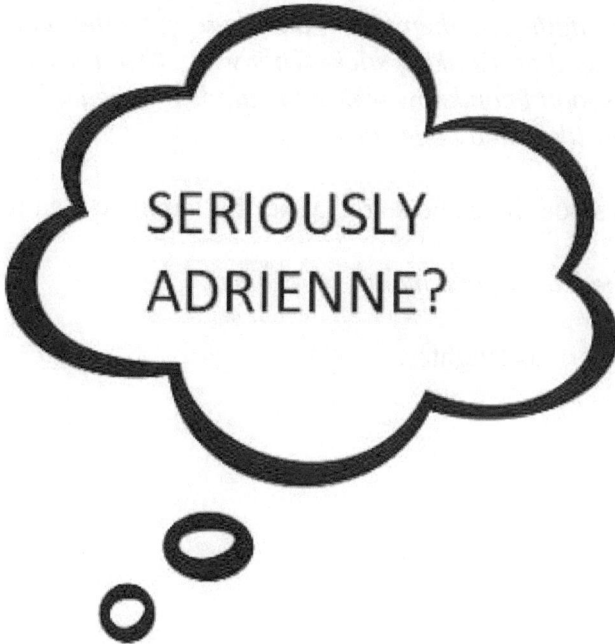

SERIOUSLY ADRIENNE?

Here is the most recent example.

We are pretty decadent when it comes to baking around here, so when butter went on sale in November, we bought eight pounds of it in preparation. There were a few pounds left over after the holiday baking was completed so they ended up as toast or sandwich spread instead of margarine. I am pretty vigilant about making sure that if you use the last of something you make sure you replace it, so a couple of weeks ago I took out a new pound of butter and cut it to place a portion in the butter dish I had just emptied and washed so it would be soft for the next person.

"Mom, you cut the butter wrong."

Apparently in all my fifty-nine years of living no one has ever trained me in the proper way to cut butter.

"You have to open the package all the way, mark it with the knife length-wise then turn it and do it again then cut it that way. So that it's like a stick. That way, when I need one tablespoon I can know where to cut, or if I need a half a cup I know it's exactly one stick".

I just stood there and stared at her for a minute then replied...

"I'll be leaving in a month, Adrienne".

Cue glorious laughter.

Should I Tell Her?

Adrienne picked up a second-hand TV over the holidays because with my sleeping space in the living room it makes it kind of awkward if she wants to play Xbox at 2 am because she can't sleep. It's a shame we didn't think of it sooner because in a sense it's now equipped like a two bedroom apartment (my room is way bigger and has a fireplace because, well, it's the LIVING ROOM) with each of us being able to settle in for the night with me watching British crime series on Netflix and her watching The Simpsons while she plays WOW...and I'm a little bit nerdy cooler because I know what that means.

This weekend I really wasn't feeling well so my trip to Barrie had to be cancelled. The two of us were in our own spaces watching what we wanted to watch, with me being miserable drinking tea hacking up a piece of lung in mine and her enjoying being able to avoid that particularly lovely experience by staying in hers.

This afternoon I was sitting here being less miserable (thank goodness!) and I heard things rattling around in the kitchen. After a bit I decided to break the cone of silence and ask...

"Whatcha doin' in there Adrienne?"

"I'm making cupcakes".

Adrienne loves to bake. It's one of those things that gives her pleasure, and it's one of the things she does spontaneously when she's happy. There she was in the kitchen, measuring and beating and pouring and I could feel it, the hum of how she was feeling flowing into me. She came out a couple of times to show me funny things on her phone or to sit cross-legged on the back of the couch for a

137

few minutes chatting. She was on a roll so she decided to put supper together while she was in there.

"Can I put a bit of this liqueur into the icing Mom? It's only going to be me and you eating it. Speaking of which I hope Elliott doesn't change his mind at the last minute and want a Bakugan cake. How would you decorate a Bakugan cake anyway? Should I just make the whole box of pasta so we can have leftovers?"

As I was sitting there, I felt my spirit lifting up, lightening in a way it hasn't in a while in this trip we're on, and I felt such incredible joy when I realized what was happening.

She was sparkling.

It's a special thing that happens, and that is the word that is closest to what it looks and feels like to those around her. Since this whole mess started, she's been happy at times, for sure. She's enjoyed life, enjoyed her family, enjoyed her friends. She's celebrated beginnings and endings, been excited at amazing Christmas present finds. Sung a little, danced a little, laughed a little. But this is the first time in a very long time that I've felt her sparkle.

Should I tell her? Is it one of those things that if I point it out it will dull it somehow?

I'll have to hope not, because she's been following this tale along with the rest of you. So hey, Adrienne...thanks for sharing with me today. I love you most the end I win.

Collateral Damage

Cancer changes people, and cancer also changes the people supporting the people who have cancer. It's something I heard before going through this experience and I am proof positive that it's an actual thing. It's sort of like collateral damage. Adrienne got a bomb tossed at her and when it exploded there I was, standing beside her, getting hit with some random debris.

One of the hits I took was to my filter. I used to have a REALLY strong one, like a five second delay that gets put in place by censors to ensure that nipple slips or the seven words you can't say on television don't get aired on live broadcasts. I would be able to have a thought, analyze it a bit to see if it was appropriate to move from brain to mouth, and act accordingly. It has helped me in many a challenging situation, like not verbally bitch slapping a bigot or turning the air blue when I'm around my grandchildren if I stub my toe or put my phone in the washing machine. Now, I'm a little bit leery of my ability to shut myself down. This morning is a perfect example of why.

Reason 652 that Adrienne needs someone with her during treatment, even the easy ones like radiation, happened over the weekend. Her lips have felt like they are on fire, and she's tried everything possible to ease the discomfort. She's very careful of products she uses on her face because of how many times she's had a bad reaction. Nothing has changed in the last little while in skin care routine or food, so we thought it was just maybe sunburn from the radiation. Then this morning she was in the bathroom and I walked in to see if she was okay and she looked at me and said...

"Mom look how swollen my lips are".

Now I was concerned because they were visibly swollen, and

139

that's very worrisome considering her allergy history. I ran through in my head the usual suspects, thinking back on what she's eaten or been exposed to over the last week outside of the radiation. mentally locating my stash of antihistamines to get her some to help reduce the reaction, knowing if she was on Benedryl she'd need more mothering because it makes you so sleepy.

You know, like a good Mom.

But here's what shot out of my mouth...

"Jesus you look like a Kardasian".

One more thing to be grateful for. I'm still allowed to live here.

You Just Couldn't Make This Shit Up

Adrienne started radiation last week, and if you've been reading along you will know that she's been having a reaction to something that is making her lips looking like a bad lip job. She woke up this morning, twenty-four hours into a Benedryl cycle, and she still looks like a Kardasian.

The radiation clinic uses state-of-the-art technology and one newer system is called an Active Breathing Coordinator. The purpose is to have the patient hold their breath to a specific volume of lung expansion to get the heart out of the line of the radiation treatment, thereby preventing heart damage, particularly in breast cancer patients whose left breast was the affected one. To do that Adrienne has a snorkel-like device in her mouth and a nose clip to prevent air from leaking out (and to prevent breath cheating) during treatment through which a measured flow of air is given then shut off. They determined exactly how much by doing a test run before she started. Once the air is shut off Adrienne needs to hold her breath until the treatment is finished, usually about twenty seconds max. The whole contraption looks like this...

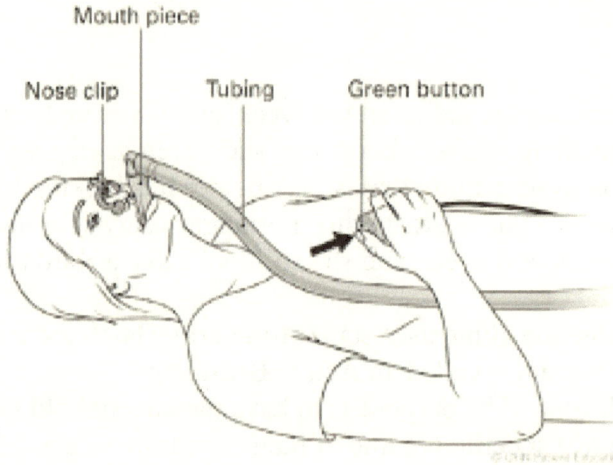

Mouth piece

Nose clip   Tubing   Green button

They were trying to figure out yesterday what might be causing the lip problem. It was possible it was the radiation but since it's really not directed at her head it was unlikely. The guess was that although they had never seen it before she might be reacting to the mouthpiece. Adrienne is allergic to soy and a lot of medical devices are being made out of bio plastics so maybe...? This could especially be a first case because most people in the age category they typically see in radiation clinics tend not to have soy allergies, which is why they couldn't rule it out as a cause in her case.

She's a little bit fed up with being the first in so much of this. First in her family...first they've seen so young...first to take the perfection away from this new contraption forever. I told her that she's done too well and the universe thinks it can keep tossing more at her.

"YOU WON'T BREAK ME UNIVERSE!" she yelled.

But still...enough already.

Last night she was very uncomfortable. Her lips felt like they were on fire even after the drugs and applying single ingredient lip stuff, and at her Aunt Paula's suggestion I offered her an ice pack. We have a ton of small ones from when she had to bring home fertility drugs and we have one already wrapped in piece of cloth for just such instances. She put it on and felt instant relief and we were both really grateful it had worked.

She knew she would need something cheesy for supper because Benedryl gives her the grunchies so we stopped by the grocery store on the way home from radiation to pick up some flatbreads. I popped into her room around suppertime to see if she thought she could actually bite them or if she wanted me to cut them up a la Elliott and here is the vision I saw.

Adrienne, an ice pack wrapped in a napkin secured to her face by a flowery headband wrapped around her head, playing video games. I begged her to let me take a picture, but she said no. Four times I asked, each time narrowing the potential audience, and each time she said no. That's how ridiculous it looked. I'm sitting here giggling a bit at the memory.

This morning on the way to the clinic we were talking about possible solutions if it turned out to be the mouthpiece. This was a serious conversation.

Adrienne...

"*I was thinking about it Mom and they could just use a condom. It's the perfect shape. Just slide that sucker on and clip the end off. I don't care I just need a barrier between it and my lips*".

Me...

"They could. Or a rubber glove. You know you aren't allergic to those and they those available."

Adrienne...

"Yeah but that's not the right shape. That's why a condom would be such a good choice."

Me..

"I know but I can't see them wanting to use one of those. But hey wait a minute!! What about those sleeves they put on the wands for vaginal ultrasounds! Those are the right shape, too, right?"

Adrienne...

"For sure and we know we have lots of those in the hospital. I had to do that enough times."

When I told her Aunt Paula about this conversation, she said if they used a condom they could at least make it neon coloured and edible. Adrienne wants tropical fruit.

You just couldn't make this shit up.

Always the Overachiever

Today was the start of week three of radiation. The Kardasian lips are still with us, so it's lots of Benedryl and ice packs on the face on a continuous basis. It's a good look...

Every Monday is x-ray day, when they hook Adrienne up to the ABC machine and get her to do the breath hold just to make sure everything is still where it's supposed to be and no changes have happened that would require an alteration to the treatment plan. It happens in the same room as the radiation does so they hook her up as usual and step out before they zap her.

The ABC has a thing that looks like a dead man's device on a bomb that Adrienne holds during treatment (I watch too much Criminal Minds) that has a green button at the end. It's important because once things are set she's alone in there and if need be she can use it to communicate with the staff that she needs them to come in by pressing the button twice, sort of like a Bat Signal.

I think it would be so cool if they actually did do that, and one of the parts of the protocol was the staff member having to don a black cape before coming and then asking in a deep tortured voice...

"I am Batman. What do you need, Patient X?"

Today as she was laying there the tube that goes from the machine to the mouthpiece somehow detached itself from the machine. As a result the air couldn't be stopped as it needs to be once her lungs are properly expanded, as per the tests they did at the beginning, so that the system knows it's time to start the process. The tube was just hanging there, waving about above her head, so she pressed the button twice as she had been taught. The technician walked in and said…

"Well, that's a first. That's never happened before".

Of course it's never happened before. Adrienne has never undergone radiation treatment before.

First to have cancer. First to be allergic to the mouthpiece. First time the tube has detached. Adrienne has always been an overachiever, but this being the first at things is getting a bit ridiculous.

Except for beating cancer the first time. She can overachieve at that to her heart's content.

Relativity Has Different Lenses Part Deux

Half way through radiation...meaning three weeks to go in the long ass trek of treatment for the monster. There are still more things to come, like continuing Herceptin and making decisions about how to suppress Adrienne's ovaries until she wants to/is allowed to get pregnant (more on that later). But the actual treatment phase that started last May is coming to an end. So, time for a little reflection I guess.

There are days in your life that become what was before and what came after days, because they usually bring a huge change in who you are or what your life will be moving forward. Things like graduation day, wedding day, baby being born day. March 15, 2019 is one of those days. That's the day I heard "Mom, it's cancer"...worst case scenario become manifest. I had no idea at the time just how much the diagnosis would change my daughter's life, and therefore mine, but I knew that it was going to be a lot.

Looking back over the last almost a year, though, there is one thing that has emerged that I also could not have predicted. In the worst-case scenario, there was a best case scenario.

Our family was in position that I could leave my job and move here to help her throughout the process, and the cherry on top is the unbelievable blessing of my job being held for me for when I go back.

Adrienne's job offered her a very generous sick leave benefit, which allowed her to meet all her financial obligations for the first six months. For the rest of the time, she fully qualified for medical unemployment insurance benefits and while it took a long time to come through, she had managed things well and was able to hang on until it did.

She had to have a second surgery in May because of some concern about the margins from the first one, but that allowed the time necessary for her to go through the fertility preservation egg retrieval treatments. That would not have been able to happen if the second surgery hadn't been necessary.

She had to undergo some horrific chemotherapy treatments, but they worked...the first time. I know of several women for whom that is not the case, and they have faced repetitions of The Awful finger breaking routine again and again.

When she was feeling well, I had a place to go that was full of love and care and fun. If I couldn't be home, it was definitely the loveliest alternative to home. When I was leaving the car here, there is a very simple and comfortable train system that lets me get there safe and sound. Perfect.

Her reproductive system did, indeed, kick back in. The hilarity of its timing, the day after she had surgery, will mean that she will know beyond any shadow of a doubt exactly when her periods came back. The menopause was not permanent, so for her no more hot flashes, no more night sweats...I'm so jealous.

I could seriously go on and on. But what it boils down to is this.

Relatively speaking, things have gone pretty well. It could have been so much worse.

Don't get me wrong, this was terribly unfair, and I am still full of rage that my child had to go through all this. I struggle to sympathize with people who have other issues that for them are the worst possible thing, wanting to say "Well at least it's not cancer." I get very frustrated when people waste their time and energy on stuff that just doesn't really matter, even though I can acknowledge for them that in their lives right now it's a really big deal. I am hopeful that once the anger dissipates, I'll be able to shift my thinking to a more compassionate path, but I just don't know if that will happen.

Because relatively speaking, even though I thought I always believed this to be true, there is a different degree of desperation for me now in appreciating that...

Every=Moment Counts^2

Wait...What?

Adrienne and I have known from the outset that she is very young to have been diagnosed with breast cancer. Every single medical professional would comment on it, ask about family history or other risk factors, and it got to the point that I really wanted to say to them...

"It's all in her file. Read it. You are asking these questions for your own sake, to appease your curiosity, and they are of no benefit to her or the treatment you're providing. Please consider that she knows she is young, she is suffering anyway, and making those types of comments actually are like another slash in the death of a thousand cuts."

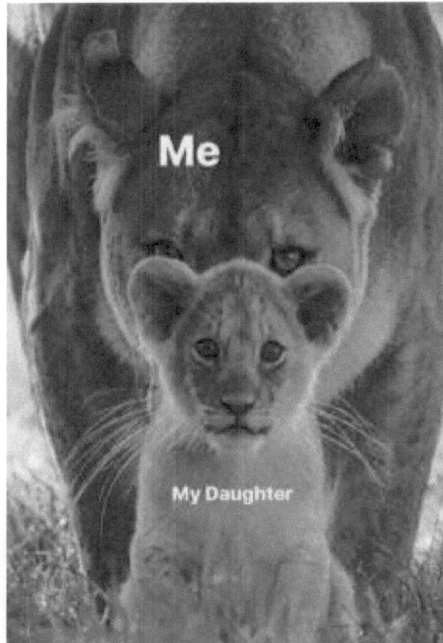

Me

My Daughter

But I didn't say it. Because doing so would also be of no benefit to my child.

The one constant from the beginning has been the shock on people's faces when Adrienne's name would be called and it would be her, not me, who got up to go into a treatment room. When she went in for surgery back in March we were sitting together in a waiting area and she was in a hospital gown, hospital slippers, a hospital blanket around her shoulders and when they came to get her for the pre-surgical dye injection into her breast the technician said...

"Who is the patient?"

Wait...what?

It's been a very obvious thing in the radiation waiting room. I can look around and see the puppy dog tilt of people's heads when she gets up, because they are trying to reconcile what they are seeing. For the vast majority of the cases of mother and daughter waiting together it's the mother who gets up, and I see the shift in their faces when Adrienne stands up and leaves me sitting there. The mothers stare at her, their eyes following her as she walks away, and then they turn and look at me. And most of the time I have to look away.

You see, they know what she is going through, what she has gone through, and I know that they can't imagine what it must have been like for me, what it must be like, to watch her suffer that way. They have had the surgery. They have walked in the shadow of The Awful. They have lost their hair, felt their muscles ache, struggled to keep food down. They have felt it all, and been so grateful it was them, and not their child.

I can see that they want to ask the questions. I can see that they want to know. But they don't ask. They just send waves of sympathy in my direction, offering me an extra boost of strength to get through one more day. I think maybe they hold their daughters a little bit closer the next time they embrace, the bubble of innocence that it can't happen to the child they would die for burst by the courageous young woman they stared at that day.

I hope they do. I really hope they do.

The Adrienne Quest

When Adrienne was first diagnosed there were so many people who felt helpless who really needed to do something. My mother gave all of us love, roots and wings and we definitely spread them when our lives offered us the opportunity, and that means that geography has been a pretty big deal for my siblings from the outset.

We were both blessed to have had my children Stephanie and Isabelle so close. Marilyn, who has been their Mom replacement for a very long time, was also on my speed dial, someone who Adrienne would feel comfortable wiping her butt if it came down to that. The woman who married my older brother, my sister in love and spirit if not in blood, the one who said neon flavoured condoms were a must, was ready to get on a plane at any time. My other brother and his wife, I know, would have been here if I needed them. I don't think any of them will ever know what it meant to have them a heartbeat away, for me to know if I couldn't, I mean really couldn't, I had others who could.

My sister in Vancouver was one of the people who really needed to do something. I cannot honestly remember how the whole thing started, because I was so wrapped up in helping Adrienne deal with what was going on, but I'll try to explain, from my perspective, what it was like to experience my child being on the receiving end of so much generosity.

One of the things that happened to Adrienne during chemotherapy, as happens to most women undergoing breast cancer treatment, is that she lost her hair. Thankfully nowadays there are multiple ways for those who are in that situation to wear head coverings that are pretty and reflect their personalities. Adrienne is a magician at scarf tying, and so my sister decided to start The Adrienne Quest to receive donations of scarves that she could send across the country so that Adrienne could always have something new and pretty to put on her head.

My sister has a network of friends, which is always lovely, but in this case they proved to be a treasure trove. My sister would carefully iron the scarves and place them in envelopes for Adrienne to open each week so that to try to ease the dread of going to chemo she'd have a special treat to open before she left. Sometimes, more often than not as the Quest continued, it would be two envelopes, one to open on chemo day and one to open when she just needed a lift. It was simply amazing, the support reaching out from strangers to help someone they had never met but they knew was going through the worst. Adrienne would light up when there was an envelope in the mailbox, gleefully opening it as we prepared to go to chemo.

Because of their generosity it got to the point that Adrienne had more scarves than she would ever need, so she made the decision to pay it forward. She found some instructions online, printed them up, put them in individual ziploc bags with some of the scarves she had received and placed them in a basket in the chemo clinic for others to be able to take home. She knew what it was like to need to feel pretty, to look in the mirror and see at least a semblance of what she was used to seeing, to see her.

This past Tuesday was a Herceptin treatment day, so once again we were back in the oncology clinic. Much to Adrienne's joy, there was a woman sitting across from us wearing something she had brought in. Someone else who needed to feel pretty, to walk confidently into the clinic knowing she looked her best. Adrienne didn't pay it forward to receive anything, but she certainly got a thrill from knowing her choice was making a difference.

This week my sister and Adrienne talked and Adrienne told her that with her hair coming back the need for scarves isn't there, but could they maybe consider continuing the Quest and providing them to a local treatment center if she provided the instructions to go with the scarves. We're not sure if it will happen, but chances are there may be an Adrienne Quest 2. I think when I get home there will likely be an Adrienne Quest 3. Who knows, maybe there is a 4, 5, 6 to infinity and beyond out there.

Thanks, Fran...little did you know what your need to feel less helpless may have started.

A Taste of What May Come

For my birthday last month, my family all pitched in to buy
me a pampering spa package. Do they know me or what?
Adrienne asked the shop owner to wait before sealing the
envelope so she could include the tip so I did have to worry
about anything. My children are simply fantastic
people. The appointment was booked for today since it's in
Toronto and Adrienne tried her best to plan it based on when
I'd want to go to Barrie. She drove me there and picked me
up and made sure what we are having for dinner today is a
non-cooking event so I'd be able to continue the pampering
all day long. Right now, I'm sitting watching an Australian
mini series on Netflix with a fire in the fireplace and a
Kilkenny in the glass. I think we're having irresistible
cookies for dessert...those Pilsbury holiday ones that when
they come out of the oven warm you just can't get enough of
them...if you're me that is. This is a beautiful day.

I heard from the owner of the spa as she was taking care of
my hands that when Adrienne bought the gift certificate she
said I had been staying with her a few months to take care of
her and a day of pampering was the least she could do. The
owner is a warm woman with a great spiritual presence, so in
the course of us chatting as she was working, I told her the
story of why.

Her son is 27 years old, and the only way I can describe her
reaction is that she can't even.

I watched her face in the dim lighting of the room, saw her
need to break eye contact with me as she tried to imagine
what it must be like. She searched for words, some kind of
personal frame of reference to relate, but the truth is she just
didn't have one. The only thing she could come up with was
her son's heart being broken from a nasty engagement ending
and how hard it was to see him go through so much anguish,

and she acknowledged that as an example of a mother wanting to take away their child's pain that was the equivalent of a drop of rain in an ocean compared to mine.

That's when I saw her lip start to quiver.

I looked at her and said...

"No, you can't go there. Because I can't go there."

And we started to talk about Kobe Bryant's passing because her niece is married to Steph Curry and her son and Curry had a shoe line that sold out of Footlocker in a heartbeat and the troubles of the millenial generation in getting a foothold on life and how all of them are working very hard and seemingly not able to get ahead and how financial experts say the biggest mistake my generation is making is supporting their children for too long by sacrificing their retirement funds and...

Anything to not go there.

I realized today that I have been pretty insulated this last ten months. With the exception of my Costco departure the people I have been exposed to, have had to speak to, have had to relate to, all know, and so they have gotten past their own need to process my experience. What occurred today was such a good thing to have happen now, because it has prepared me for what may come.

There are a lot of people back home who love me, who never had a chance to share their grief for me face to face, who have daughters Adrienne's age or close to it. People who can't even. So I need to be prepared for that when I encounter them for the first time, for shutting it down on both sides. At least until I have a chance to get on the other side of it myself. Because today was a very VERY close call.

So here's my plan. How about those (insert sports team here). I hope it works.

The Return

One of the amazing things that has happened in my life since all this started is that the Rancho Cucamonga Public Library made the decision to keep my job open until I got back. As many of my readers are Canadian you may not realize the significance of this decision, and how it made me feel. Part time staff have very little legislative rights in the US. They don't get paid for holidays. They are mostly at the mercy of their employers when it comes to hours and benefits. But this place, my first job once I got my Green Card, the one I really wanted, is letting me come back. At first it was six months leave, then eight, and in in the end it will be a bit more than nine, and they still are letting me come back. Who does that?

The Rancho Cucamonga Public Library, that's who.

My boss communicated with me this week to let me know that there are discussions being held about my return and they hope to have a schedule for me within a week or two. I stared at that comment for a second. It's funny, I think I thought that I'd just be filling in open spots as they came up. Hadn't occurred to me that the library would give me a regular schedule, would do what they could to make my work life as close to what it was before as they are able given budgets and availability. Who does that?

The Rancho Cucamonga Public Library, that's who.

I feel like the library will be a huge anchor as part of my healing process. It's familiar and the staff are so caring and I love the community a lot. I have that vision of walking through the door and putting on my librarian suit of armor as I pass (I AM BATMAN), that persona that allows me to fill up my soul a bit every day. That gets to thrill at finding that "book with the blue cover and the blond girl" because I am magic with Google. To watch the face of the child who is panicking about a report relax as I give them a much less painful alternative read. To get hugs from the little people, to hear them call "Miss Debbie" across a parking lot, to see them struggle when they see me anywhere else because what am I doing outside the library?

My boss asked me how I'm feeling about coming back to the library. I'm ecstatic...I'm anxious...I'm curious...I'm grateful...I have so many feelings about coming back. I'm different in many ways and I'm afraid that the snapshot in time that people remember me from may have to be adjusted a bit. But I also know that my coworkers are the most fantastic people and I couldn't be luckier in having them waiting there. I know I'm going to have to be prepared for the emotion I'll feel when they hug me, because so many of them are mothers and I know they can't even. And I also can't wait for the wonder of the newer staff about who the heck is this woman?

We will see. But one thing I know for sure is that it's going to feel like being home. And I'm going to need that feeling as much as possible as I try to find my balance. And who will have the compassion to ease me through that?

The Rancho Cucamonga Public Library, that's who.

I am one lucky girl.

PS...If you're my coworker and you're reading this, I got kinda fat. You're allowed to notice.

The Return Part Deux

I was having a bit of a lie in this morning. Since I woke up at 7 am I think I can say not as lazy of a lie in as others I've had, but still...

My mind is like one of those memes you see where the brain keeps people awake by going into high gear at bedtime, except mine kicks in much more in the mornings when I'm alone in the quiet. My nighttime thoughts end up in my dreams and those have been SUPER intense and weird lately. Like the one I had where there was wheat growing out of my arms and everyone was freaking out but I was fine, showing them how I could pluck it out to harvest it and my arm would return to normal. Googled that and man, was it on the money. Wheat takes a lot of time and effort to grow and having a healthy crop at the end is a big accomplishment. No difficulty at all figuring out that symbolism.

My morning brain kicked in this morning looking around the room. This has been my home for almost a year. And I started wondering how Adrienne would feel looking at my corner and finding it empty. Permanently empty on a full-time live-in mother basis. We have so successfully navigated this experience that although I know beyond any shadow of a doubt that there will be such joy at getting her home back (Mom I love you but I'm really over you...Don't worry Adrienne I'm really over you, too) I also know that, like me, being away from each other is going to start the process of lifting the cover off the box.

At the very beginning of this whole shitstorm Adrienne talked to me about how she didn't know how she would deal with the end of the intensive phase of treatment. This has been her life, and it has been my life, for almost a year. Everything, and I mean EVERYTHING, has had to be filtered through the fact that she had cancer. I know for me it's going to be so difficult. I have had the chance to go to Barrie to see my family there, but only if everyone there was healthy because I couldn't bring back a virus. And if there was a virus there, I had to choose between my children. I couldn't plan more than a few days in advance because I didn't know if she'd be okay to be alone but thankfully Stephanie and Scott didn't need more notice than "Hey can you pick me up on the 5:26 train?". I bought my return ticket to California, but I was terrified to tell anyone about it in case I jinxed it somehow. Even now I think I'll believe I'm going home when I get on the plane. I have no idea how long it's going to take for me to think I get to stay there.

People have been saying that there's support out there, but we have learned along the way that there isn't a lot available for people like us. Adrienne is an outlier, and as such I am also an outlier. I'm the mother of a 28-year-old woman who had breast cancer and is in remission. Her challenges have been similar to others with cancer but at the same time so so different. Of course, there are women like her out there, mothers like me, but we are still in the shadows. Even though through all the treatment she's been through she's shone, something will always happen that makes us take a step back out of the light to keep us safe.

I am not sure how I will deal with the end of treatment, either. I'd like to come out of the shadows, I really would. But I think it will be a while before I relax enough to step out into the sun. Baby steps, I think. I'll keep you posted.

It's Just...A Lot

I went up to Barrie this past weekend, my last visit before I head home this week. It left Adrienne on her own for a few days, the day after she finished the six weeks of radiation treatment, which with a few exceptions means the end of the plan of attack she started last May. She's in remission, a razor thin edge of a state of calm. I don't know if it's fully settled in for either of us.

While I was away, she did some Spring cleaning, went to visit a friend, baked some cupcakes, and had a moment. A moment where she realized that she can put the weight down.

It's been a very heavy burden, this thing she's been carrying. There has been a lot of people in her corner, a lot of people waiting to lift her up if she stumbled, but like those athletes who scream out 'DON'T TOUCH ME' so they can crawl across the finish line on their own, she has carried this load. And right now, I'm not sure exactly who she carried it in such a dignified matter for.

Did she do it to represent her generation, the generation so many people shit on? She was like a lone wolf in every circumstance she encountered, and as such there was a constant spotlight on her to see how she'd manage it all. At one point another cancer patient told her that she had been an inspiration to her as she began her own cancer experience. It was lovely to hear that, but in hindsight I'm wondering if that added a few more stones to the pile.

Did she do it for her friends, whose mortality got slammed down on the table in front of them like an angry fist by her diagnosis? Every time she encountered them, she had her best game face on, never letting them into the darkness she woke up into every day. And every time she had plans she'd have to cross her fingers that she would be able to make it, and I am pretty sure she pushed herself a couple of times to get there so they wouldn't know how bad things actually were.

Did she do it for her sisters, who love her like only sisters can? Stephanie told me this weekend that she *knows* it was bad, but she never had to experience how bad, because Adrienne made a special effort to be herself when she was in Barrie, especially with the little ones. She played video games with Elliott, went to the park with Clara, and then would crawl into her shell to recuperate as soon as we got back to Toronto.

Did she do it for her Dad, who stayed alone in California so that I could be here with her through it all? She has always been a Daddy's girl, and I know how hard it was for him to be so far away while she was going through all this, so when they were together they'd still have a glass of wine and make fun of me like they always do. I know she didn't want him staying here during The Awful because she knew she couldn't put on the face and she knew she'd try to do it for him.

Did she do it for me?

This one is the hardest for me to contemplate, that my presence here, although needed and welcomed, added to the pile. I have always been the rock of the family, but there were some chips and cracks that showed along the way this past year. I know she is used to seeing me as a person, but I'm not sure if it was fully acknowledged prior to now that I actually had a breaking point. I know I have done my utmost to hide it from them over the years. When they would leave me to go home or back to school, I would tear up a bit but then pull it back until the door closed behind them at which point I'd cry my eyes out. There isn't a lot of ways to hide in a one-bedroom apartment that you share everything in, and with the emotional connection we have did she hold back from telling me how she was feeling to protect me?

Or did she do it for her, because she knew that coming out the end of it all she'd have to live with how it went for the rest of her life, and she used all of these pieces at her disposal to create a safe place, a shield from the pain that would sometimes try to swamp her. When she was starting to feel her muscles quiver, starting to think she couldn't do it anymore, couldn't hold it up, were all of these people and their energy a source of power to take one more step, get through one more day? I hope so much that this is the truth of the matter. It is so much easier for me to think that it is.

She told me last night that her moment, realizing she could put the weight down, was a really big one. And she also knows that she'll have to put it down painfully slowly, one stone at a time, to make sure it doesn't, in the end, put her down to the ground. Watching for triggers, forgiving herself for the anger slipping out, giving herself space to breathe in her new reality. Because, ya know, in her own words from the very beginning of this....

It's just a lot.

The End...

Souvenirs

So, I'm home. Back in California in my lovely apartment sleeping on my own bed. Has it sunk in yet? Nope. I'm giving that some time and giving myself total control over how and when that happens, plus a lot of forgiveness for not being over the moon about being here. Don't get me wrong, I am so happy to be in my own space. It was so lovely walking in here last night and seeing things that I had left, that some might consider needed to be put away, exactly where they had been when I left. The fabric softener is the wrong brand, but I can fix that next time it's purchased. The coffee tastes different, but I'll adjust. I have a mountain of mail to go through, a bunch of decisions about clothes and shoes. But I look over and see all my memories still on the walls...the souvenirs of a life well traveled and well lived. I'll get there, in time.

Adrienne and I had a little talk in San Francisco about the experience. She said that she thought my recovery would be so much different from hers because so much of what she had to deal with was physical and all of mine was psychological, and those can be a little more tricky to manage. I have no scars that can be seen, as she does. We got tattoos the last day of radiation to commemorate the end of treatment and mine is very visible and in my face and hers is tucked under the breast that took her down this terrible road. She'll see it often enough, but she couldn't deal with looking down at her arm as she was typing up a work report and having a reminder of what this last year has been like. She did the math and realized that six percent of her life has been lost dealing with cancer. Six percent. That's a pretty big number.

I could see that stuff was bubbling to the surface, a trickle of lava coming through the cracks, under so much pressure from having been held in for so long. Could see the look on her face as she reminisced. Could feel the anguish, the disbelief still. But she held it back, as she has done so many times. That is, until about ten minutes before we landed.

She turned to me and in a very excited for me voice said…

"Mom, you get to go home. You're home".

We held hands as I looked out the window and saw the lights of my city come into view, trying to figure out how I was feeling. And I felt her start to shake. And then I heard her crying. Not slow tears, but an eruption of uncontrolled out loud sobbing. I pulled her into my arms and held her as she wept into my shoulder. She fought hard to bring it back, but in that moment, it was so much bigger than her. When she finally did get it under control, I asked her if she knew what triggered it.

"You get to go home, Mom. And if you get to go home, that means I'm done."

Because I told her I would stay with her until treatment finished, to make sure if she needed me I was there, and me being willing and ready to go home represented so much more than just packing up and getting on a plane. It means she really, truly, gets her life back. There is still more. This will never be over. But the worst of it most certainly is.

And I know, Adrienne, that your experience will be much more tricky than mine because you have both. You have the physical scars, the constant reminders, and you also have the deep torturous emotional horror and terror on top of that. Souvenirs of six percent of your life.

So many souvenirs...

Going Public...A Little

Big sports winners have made this the cliche answer to "How are you going to celebrate your win?"

"I'M GOING TO DISNEYLAND!!"

Adrienne is not a big sports winner, but I think her victory is much more significant. She beat back cancer, badass thing that she is. And since Disneyland is my happy place, it made perfect sense that when she came back to California with me for a quick holiday that we would go there. Disneyland is expensive, but I have an annual pass and we have a magical Disney fairy in our lives, so the cost wasn't a factor. And even if our fairy couldn't have sprinkled fairy dust on us, I would have spent the money. Some things are just worth it.

Disneyland gives out buttons near the entrance at City Hall that say things like First Visit or It's My Birthday or I'm Celebrating. Staff have a Sharpie marker that they use to write down details like names or dates so they are an excellent free souvenir. About an hour into the park and at the very furthest point from the entrance Adrienne said "Oh we should have gotten buttons, Mom! We're definitely celebrating today". But because I am a Disneyland frequent flyer I know that most of the shops in the park have buttons in their drawers under the cash register so while she waited in line for A Small World I hopped over to the shop by the exit to see if I could pick up a couple.

I knew what Adrienne wanted hers to say, but I had to think for a few minutes as I was waiting my turn to speak to the cashier about what I would put on mine. What was I actually celebrating today? And then it came to me clear as day. Here is what our buttons look like...

Adrienne has very rarely been public about her cancer battle. She is all about social media like so much of her generation but she chose to keep most of the details of the last year out of that part of her life. With her permission it has been me who has revealed the nitty gritty details through this ongoing story. So, it was very interesting to see her make the choice yesterday to put her victory on such public display. She wore the button front and center and the contrast between the colour of the button and what she was wearing made it catch the eye as glances drifted over us while we waited in line. Some people looked at it, looked at her, and looked away. But there were enough, more than enough, who took that next step and said this...

"Congratulations. That is definitely something to celebrate".

Strangers look at her and think she looks great. Her makeup is on point, her hair is a gorgeous colour, her eyes are bright, she's beautifully dressed. But she is reminded every single day of the impact cancer has had. All she has to do is look in the mirror. She can hide her scars and weird tan lines from the radiation with strategic clothing choices, but there is one thing she can't do anything about.

While she is celebrating beating cancer this public gesture was also a way to say "What you see was not my choice. My hair was taken, not given". And when they look at her after reading the button, you can see it reflected in their faces, the understanding.

Taken, not given. A very important distinction.

Right When She Needed It Most

Yesterday was a magical day. The weather was brilliant, a perfect California Spring day that was an unexpected but so welcome gift in February. The drive up from Anaheim to Manhattan Beach was easy and relaxed, even though I had to take two of the worst freeways in Southern California to get here. We got to the hotel two hours before check in time but our room was ready, so we were able to unpack the car and head down to the beach for the walk down to the pier. But as amazing at all of that was, those things are not what made yesterday so full of magic.

Adrienne woke up not feeling very good about herself yesterday. It happens, when the physical effects of the treatment make her struggle with her appearance as we go out to face the world. And her body was telling her that two days of walking around theme parks was a bit much considering how little exercise she's been able to do for a while. We walked down to the beach for the trek to the pier but about halfway there she had to head back up to the walkway because the angle of the shore was causing her to hurt. I selfishly stayed by the water, as she encouraged me to do, because she knows it heals me. We met back up at the base of the pier and started the climb up the hill to wander through the shops as we spent time waiting to go to dinner, and it was a tough walk. We didn't go into any shops until we were at the top (I'm only climbing this hill ONCE, Mom) and that's where it started.

"Oh my God I love your earrings|? Where did you get those, they're so gorgeous!!"

"What a lovely dress! Perfect for a day like this!"

"Your necklace is so pretty; the design is amazing."

"I have to ask you...where did you get your haircut? Your hair is SO beautiful."

That last one created a bit of a moment where I had to step in and rescue her by saying it was regrowth after cancer treatment. AWKWAAAARRRDDDDDD.

When I made the reservation for our dinner last night, I added a note requesting a table by the window because we were celebrating my daughter finishing nine months of cancer treatment. The tables are in high demand and I was hopeful that playing the cancer card would help us get one because I really wanted Adrienne to have that sunset. We got one, right by the window, with the sunset framed by palm trees. And then when we got the bill the restaurant had comped our appetizers and dessert. Nothing said, but recognition of the experience.

And then the cherry on top.

David Kim came for a visit. David Kim's laugh is one of the greatest gifts the universe has to offer. And she laughed so hard her lungs complained.

Such joy, right when she needed it most.

Luc's Story

I have dropped a lot of names into this story since I started it way back when. You may have noticed that one name didn't really figure into things except for a mention here and there. One person that has been an important part of this whole thing in a behind the scenes sort of way. The reality is that I just couldn't go there. I had so much going on with my day to day that imagining his life and how he was feeling was something I couldn't bring into the mix for fear of it overwhelming me.

This is Luc's story. Because now that I am home with him, I can go there a little bit.

When I got the "Mom, it's cancer" call last March 15th I was alone at home, as is the usual most Friday mornings. I never call Luc at work unless I absolutely need him for something, so when I called and he didn't respond I knew he was in a meeting. I left a message, another indication I needed him right now. How must it have been for him to hear me tearfully say "I know you're busy, but you have to call me back. Please call me back." He would have known if I couldn't hold it together it was something big. I'm sure in his wildest dreams he wasn't expecting to hear what he heard when he called me and I said, between uncontrollable sobs, that Adrienne had cancer and I needed him to come home.

"I'll be right there."

He walked back into the meeting, said his wife needed him and he was leaving. Just like that. These are important meetings that need his input, and as I knew he would he just left. That's who he is for me, for his children...the safe place that will always be right there.

He knew I would be leaving. He has known since Stephanie took her first breath that his role in the universe had taken a monumental shift. I am that kind of mother, and he has chosen to honour and support that instead of being jealous of the love I have for them, what I am willing to sacrifice for them, that I would give my life for them.

Luc has never lived alone, at least not for long. He went from home to a naval posting living on ship to moving in with me. We have no family here, friends but none like the close ones we have in Canada. So me leaving meant he was going to be alone. So very alone, and for a very long time. And what did he constantly say to me during all this time?

"I'm so glad you can be with her."

I'm so glad you can be with her. She needs you. It's the most important job you have right now. Don't worry about me.

Luckily for us Luc's job gave him a lot of flexibility to work from home over the summer when he wasn't required at the office and he was able to come up to Canada for a week or two for visits. It was a lovely respite from his lonely life, coming home to an empty apartment night after night, week after week. But from September onward he was no longer able to be away from the office. I came back once, in September, but other than that he wasn't with us until Christmas.

I think he was hanging on with all his might until Christmas, because the plan was that I would come home with him in January. I knew before he arrived that I would have to stay through radiation, and it broke my heart knowing I would have to tell him he would have to go home alone. I think that's the only time during all this that I saw how hard it had been, the look on his face when I told him that news, because otherwise he never let it show the entire time. That look told me so much about the abyss of loneliness this had dropped him into. And my heart broke again as the unspoken message passed between us.

"I can't choose you, Luc. I have to choose her."

"I know, Debbie. I know."

Luc's story is also one of courage. The courage to be a country away from his child, because we needed his income for me to be able to do what I did. The courage to face an empty house day after day. The courage to trust that she would be okay, because he couldn't be there to protect her, or me. The courage to trust that he mattered when my world got so small that even he couldn't get in. The courage to believe that when I got back, I would be able to come all the way back, that this last year hadn't changed me so fundamentally that he wouldn't recognize me. And now the courage to understand that even though my body is here, my mind isn't, and he needs to allow me the time and space to make the trip all the way home.

So much courage...

Paula's Story

I first met Paula when I was ten. My brother John brought her home to meet his family because he had fallen head over heels, and a few months later they were married. Paula has been around for so much of my life that it's hard to remember her not being there. There are eleven years between us, and when you are ten and twenty one that's a big deal, but as we have gotten older and gone through different life phases that eleven years has gotten smaller and smaller, and now they make no difference at all. We have the same heart.

When Adrienne was looking at going to university the decision was made that she would go to Prince George where John and Paula live and stay in their basement where they set up an awesome private space with a separate entrance so Adrienne could have some independence. Paula is one of the most caring people out there, an old soul, and she would bring soup down to Adrienne when she heard her coughing, offer a glass of wine after a rough day, and in general be that person if she was needed. She did the same for Isabelle when it was her turn to go to university. Paula is the one who first said Adrienne sparkles, and her son Dave is the only one who ever was allowed to give her a nickname. She was so patient watching Adrienne grow, and laughed with me when we went to see her have puppet sex in the university play, stood proudly with me watching her graduate (finally!). There grew a great love for my children, a connection that created a greater bond between Paula and me as the years passed. How could it not. These were my babies.

As you can imagine, Adrienne's diagnosis last year hit Paula particularly hard. Yet although she struggled with her own feelings about what was happening, Paula became my person, the only person I was completely honest with the

177

entire time I was with Adrienne in Toronto. She was there for me whenever I needed her, felt guilty if she turned her phone off because she was simply exhausted and required some rest, and I think she made my brother pay attention to her phone in case it was me.

We never actually spoke. I knew I couldn't speak to her because if I did, I would lose the hard-won battle with tears. Instead, we texted. Sometimes many times a day, sometimes a few times a week, and if it had been a few days she'd always check in.

We didn't need to speak to each other, though, for me to know...

I felt her hand rubbing my back, heard her gentle sighs, knew she would study her words before she said something in return to make sure it wouldn't add to my burden. I sensed her tears but she never spoke of them unless they were happy ones. She absorbed my worries, my fears, my anger, my despair, and by sharing them with her they lessened a bit for me. How selfish of me, I know, but my burden was so big and so heavy that there were times when I feared it would overwhelm me if I had to carry it on my own. She was just there, always, holding me up. Always...

I wish for everyone going through what I have gone through that they have a Paula in their lives. I don't think I would have survived this without her.

Oh, and thanks, John for letting me borrow her. Funny, I can hear your response in my ear.

"I'm so glad she could be there for you..."

Sounds vaguely familiar.

The Return Part Trois...Real Talk

I went back to work this week.

When I went in on Monday my key card worked to open the staff door to get me inside the building. I went inside and stood for a minute, and then I started up the stairs and had to stop halfway up to take a breath. Not because of being out of shape, but because of just...being there.

It's been a long time.

I was so welcome, the staff who were working coming out to greet me and hug me and express their happiness that Adrienne is okay. One of my coworkers when she saw me came up for a hug and said she was so glad to see me because it meant if I was back that my daughter was doing well. Anything I need, just let them know. Take your time. We're here for you. It was exactly the type of compassion and caring that I remember, one of the reasons I was so grateful to be able to go back to my job. Everyone has asked how I am doing.

How am I doing. I would really appreciate it if someone could help me figure out the answer to that question.

I recently saw a Criminal Minds episode (told you I watch too much Criminal Minds) where the perpetrator was hallucinating that there was an alternate parallel universe that he needed to get to. There was a character from there that he could talk to but when he would try to get there he would run into something like one of those force fields where poking it is like dropping a pebble into water. It's perfectly clear but as real as a brick wall.

That's as close as I can come to how I'm doing.

Almost a year ago I was thrust into an alternate universe. My whole world changed, my focus on one thing and one thing only: making sure Adrienne was okay. I've written about how cancer does that, becomes the center of everything you think, everything you do, a filter that everything is run through. I lived, breathed, ate, slept the fight against a cancer that could take my child. And although I can leave some of that behind now, I'm struggling. I'm really struggling.

So much of what I love, the people I love, are on the other side of that wall. I can see them. I can communicate with them. I can feel their support reaching out to me. I can reach through and hold Luc's hand, feel his patience, his love, but he is still on the other side. The truth is that I've been *here* for so long that I'm finding it terribly difficult to get *there*. It's like I'm watching myself going through my days, among them, but not among them.

It's only been a few weeks. That's what I keep telling myself. Be easy on yourself, you've been through a nightmare. But right this very minute what I want most in the world is to hug my daughter because she's on this side with me. The only one who is. The only person I can be with where my feelings are normal. The only person who is with me in this unspoken horror story of what has been, where neither of us has to say anything to know.

That this was just...a lot.

Souvenirs...Part Deux (WTF Universe)

I was getting ready to prepare some green beans in the kitchen yesterday when my phone told me Adrienne was requesting a video chat. I froze. In the seconds between when I saw who it was and hitting the answer button my mind raced...she hasn't had any tests recently so it can't be "Mom it's cancer" again, right?

No, Debbie, it can't be. Resume breathing.

Welcome to my world.

The face I saw when the video connected was sobbing uncontrollably, trying to bring it back enough that she could actually talk. Once again, I wished I could hug my daughter, could offer comfort for whatever it was that was tearing her apart. But I can't, so I went to that calm place, the place I've practiced and perfected for just such situations, to give her the time she needed.

"I'm here. I'm right here. Whenever you're ready."

It took her a few minutes, keening with distress, trying to catch her breath. I focused on my own breathing, my own heartbeat, centering myself in the moment. My mind had slowed but still ran through a list of possibilities. Her job?...Her car?...A really rough day?

"Mom, my eyelashes aren't just thinning. They're falling out again. And I just washed my face and a bunch of eyebrow hairs are falling out again, too. Is that normal?"

What the fuck, universe? What...the actual...FUCK!!!!!

Out of everything the eyebrow and eyelash loss was the worst, the thing she struggled with the most while she was undergoing treatment, because it gave her cancer face. The hair being taken, not given, is still a very sensitive spot, especially when people compliment her on it, but she can cover that with a beanie if she doesn't want to look at it. Not so much with her face, which was why there was such joy when her eyebrows grew back in so perfectly, when her eyelashes started to cast a shadow. In what possible scenario is it fair that she is losing them again, five months after she finished chemotherapy, when she is trying to get her life back, to establish her new normal?

While she continued to cry, I turned to Google. I knew I would get different results than she did because of the US/Canada thing. Plus she knows I can ask Google the question in such a way that I usually get the best answers. And you know what?

It's normal. For some cancer survivors there's a six week to three-month cycle of regrowth and loss that eventually settles. One more of those things no one tells you about cancer treatment. How cruel is this for women who have lost so much, suffered so much, that just when they are climbing out of the abyss, they look in the mirror and cancer has once again taken. There are enough souvenirs. It's simply not necessary to create any more.

Adrienne told me after my last entry that she had been trying to find words for how she was feeling and when she read about my invisible wall that spoke her truth. Everyone thinks it's over. Because the treatment successfully put her into full remission and she is able to go back to work they think it's over. But she is far from being over what happened to her. Far from recovering her balance from the trauma of the last year. Far from processing the anger, the fear, the despair.

"I guess in a way, Mom, losing my eyebrows and eyelashes again means that my outsides are going to be more reflective of my insides right now."

Cue my heart breaking once again. What the fuck, universe. What...the actual...fuck.

.

Cancer Bingo Anyone?

There were so many times during Adrienne's cancer experience where she said that she wished that she could just wear a sign around her neck that would appease people's curiosity or stop them from offering unsolicited advice or opinions. It's amazing how people seemed to feel that her cancer diagnosis gave them permission to judge her choices, gave them the right to tell her how she should be living. My filter was strained to the maximum holding back what I really wanted to say in response and the majority of the time I held back simply because I knew it would not be helpful to Adrienne for me to jump in. Other times it was because I was pretty certain that nothing I could say would change the speaker's opinion anyway so it was an exercise in futility.

She sent me this image this morning in a private message and with her permission I'm going to share it with you.

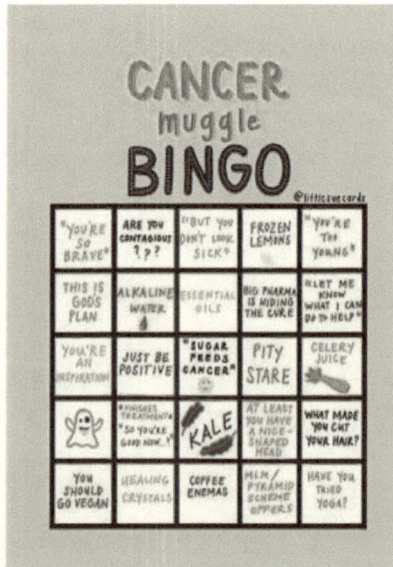

There are only a few of the squares on this bingo card that she couldn't put a marker on. People actually said these things to her, out loud. She was in a fight for her life, choking down food, trying to deal with what cancer had taken away from her, and people told her to eat kale, that she had a nicely shaped head . What is said is not what is heard, as many times it's an unfinished thought expressed. "You look great!" (for someone with cancer). "Short hair suits you" (good thing because it wasn't a choice).

I know that for some of you the idea of hearing that saying "You're so brave" or "You're an inspiration" is not what all cancer patients need to hear...10,383 times...but it's the truth.

Cancer isn't a battle that people enter into voluntarily knowing the dangers ahead. Cancer isn't a journey that people go on in the hope that they will evolve into a better version of themselves. Cancer isn't a choice. Cancer is an invader. And you can drink all the celery juice in the world and it will not stop the invader from killing you.

Lifestyle changes may, indeed, lessen your chances of getting cancer in the long run. I'm not disputing that. But at the age of twenty seven, do you really think she needed to hear that she had done something to bring this upon herself by eating too much sugar, by not eating enough kale? Because that's how those statements translate. They may be well intended, but that's the message they send.

As I am writing this I am realizing how angry I still am about how some of this made her feel. And I am also realizing that this is one of those instances where my filter is damaged, because what I have written may offend some of the people reading it and while that is not my intention the truth of the matter is I don't care. This story has always been about my truth, about her truth, and the fact that somewhere out there someone put this image together tells me that she was not alone in her feelings about this. That I was not alone.

I am not sure what the best thing is to say to someone with cancer. One of the most helpful things for her, though, was this...

"Wow...that sucks".

A very simple statement that told her that the person speaking understood. No advice, no opinion, just a statement of fact.

Cancer sucks.

The End

March 15th, 2019

It started out like any other day. I set the alarm early because I had to do a few storytimes at work and as usual hit snooze about eight times. Finally bit the bullet and threw off the covers, walked into the kitchen to pour myself a cup of coffee, and came to sit in my spot on the couch to do my normal morning routine...check banking, read email, take surveys, open Facebook, play some Candy Crush as I watched the news.

And then the phone rang.

"Mom...it's cancer."

My fingers just froze on the keyboard. Give me a minute...

I still carry some Mom-guilt that she was alone in the doctor's office when she got the news. That's how sure everyone was that it wasn't cancer. Every medical professional Adrienne came into contact with exuded certainly that it was something benign, because she was so young. I never EVER would have let her be alone if there was an inkling in my brain that the doctor would look into her beautiful young face and tell her the shocking, devastating news. The news that would change the course of the rest of her life.

I try to imagine how she must have felt when she left the office, walked down the stairs, got into her car, paid the parking attendant, turned left at the lights to head home. I know that she didn't call me until she parked in her driveway, because she knew she'd never get there if she did. I am grateful to the universe that it protected her from idiot drivers making stupid choices that she'd have had to react to on that drive since I am fairly confident she was on autopilot.

I had a flight booked on March 17th to be in Ontario for Clara's first birthday on March 18th. As I was talking to Adrienne I opened up the airline website to see if I could get there any sooner. That was the week that airlines pulled the Boeing 737 Max out of operations and there was literally no way I could get there any sooner without taking 26 hours of travel time and getting me there only ten hours sooner, so I stayed with my original plan.

My fingers keep freezing on the keyboard. I think I must have a primal memory of that time that's impacting my ability to move, to think. Need another minute...

Adrienne picked me up at the airport. She walked into my arms, I held her as she shook from head to toe, rubbed her back as we stood there. Then she pulled it back in. She had to drive us to Barrie, after all. I could have driven, but she needed to be behind the wheel to keep herself in check. To keep the feelings in the box.

Where they have been for a year.

Adrienne is struggling a lot right now, dealing with anger and fear and despair. She asked her sister Isabelle to come down this weekend so she wouldn't have to be alone today. Isabelle was woken up this morning by a house centipede crawling on her neck. Such a great gift from universe, waking up to her sister yelling and leaping around the room instead of waking up and laying alone in her bed thinking about March 15th, 2019.

Like I did. At exactly 8:30 this morning. Which is when the phone rang 365 days ago.

Need another minute...

Six Months

There have been many things impacted by the arrival of Covid 19 in North America. I know how big they are. People have lost loved ones. People are out of work. Life has come to a standstill and while there is light at the end of the tunnel the world feels like a very scary place.

And yet once again, I find myself feeling grateful.

I have mentioned in the past that breast cancer was not the first time Adrienne's life had been threatened. For the first three years of her life she was in and out of hospital to treat asthma crises. She has the disease of asthma, the kind that means that if she were born fifty years ago, she possibly wouldn't have made it out of childhood. She was a patient of the country's number one pediatric respirologist at Sick Kids in Toronto. Every new medication brought onto the market, she was one of the first to get it. And thanks to the development of these drugs, our lives changed, and she was able to live like a regular little girl...to run, to sing, to dance.

Six months ago, my child was in the midst of being treated for cancer with chemotherapy. Her immune system had been shattered by poison that was pumped into her body every week to kill the monster that was trying to take her life. Any infection, any virus that took hold in her body would have run rampant and unchallenged. So regardless of the miracle of the medications that keep her asthma at bay, that have let her live normally, Covid 19 would likely have killed her.

Her body has certainly not fully recovered from the ordeal it has been through, and so she is doing the right thing, isolating herself from the world until the crisis passes. Most importantly to her, she still has to walk into an oncology clinic every three weeks to get the game changing Herceptin treatment that is continuing the battle against her triple positive breast cancer. She knows there are people there who are where she was six months ago, and the idea that she would inadvertently expose them to Covid 19 when their bodies have nothing to fight it with horrifies her.

My experience over the last year, trying to do all I could to protect my child from things I could have some control over, has made me hyper-aware of the danger choosing not to take social distancing seriously can pose. It has made me understand very clearly that as I walk through life, I have no idea which people in my path are compromised in some way. That makes it my responsibility to assume everyone is, to take actions to protect all of them. The children...the parents...the grandparents. All of them.

My child is six months away from being completely vulnerable to this virus. I am so grateful for that distance.

Six months, my friends. Imagine how you would feel if by choosing to be out when you didn't need to be you crossed Adrienne's path as she was on her way to the hospital for life saving treatment, and you killed her.

Imagine...

The Staircase

Our world is a pretty topsy turvy place at the moment. There are many obvious side impacts of all that's going on. Mine is a very personal one.

I had a plan, you see. I have been holding on to my emotions for so long, and sometimes it felt like I was barely making it, digging in with my nails, hanging off the edge of the abyss. Coming back to California was going to give me a chance to breathe, to go sit by the ocean and just listen to it, watch the waves crash into the shore. It would get me back to my job, where I love them, and they love me. Let me release, bit by bit, the anger...the anguish...the despair...the horror.

The best laid plans of mice and men...

I have been in regular contact with my kids, both by text and video chat, and it's certainly helping with things. I have established a pretty good routine for myself...Spanish online, going for a walk as I listen to my audiobook, home to shower and make plans for supper, maybe a few loads of laundry thrown in there for good measure.

I've been here before, and I know how necessary it is for me to not get sucked into the darkness. It can be like a black hole, its gravity pulling with an incredible amount of power. I try to focus every day on how lucky my family is during this time of crisis. I try to feel the gratitude for being six months away from being terrified to my core. I try to appreciate that I have enough toilet paper to last me for a while, and that for some reason I keep running into the last package in the store. And I think I'm doing okay, until something like this happens.

This is the staircase...

It's an ordinary staircase, a way to go from Adrienne's street to the one below. It goes between some houses, has six or eight stairs alternating with a landing so you can rest on the way up. And it's where we used to walk when she had cancer.

The oncologist highly recommended that Adrienne keep active during chemo. Walking was about all she could manage, and although I knew it might be tough, I made this staircase a part of it. I'd encourage her to climb those stairs to keep her heart and lungs functioning as her body was under attack from both the illness and the cure. She was almost always up for it, pushing herself a bit sometimes. At first, she could slowly walk up all the stairs at once, but as things progressed she had to stop on every landing to catch her breath. She was determined that it would not conquer her. It was a battle she could fight and win.

Today she posted this picture because the weather is finally warm enough for her to get out for a walk and she knows this place is a good workout. I looked at it, and my heart stopped. My stomach flipped. My ears starting ringing. I was right back there, back to The Awful, back to watching her struggle to walk up six stairs.

I don't like it there. I don't want to be tossed into the abyss. I need the world to settle just for me, so I can have a chance to process some of what I am trying so desperately not to lose control of my sanity to. I am doing my best, following all the suggestions from mental health professionals, but it's just so hard. I need the time and space when the current stressful situation isn't dominating everyone's lives to help myself heal.

I have a feeling that's going to take a long time.

Relativity Has Different Lenses, Part Trois

Let me start out by acknowledging that we are all living in very difficult times. Life has been turned on its head and there really isn't a road map for how we will navigate our way through it. There are many lights, like the Hearts in the Window campaign that started out in a small town in Canada and is now is making its way around the world. There are many blessings, like the fact that each household in my family is so far still getting a paycheque and no one in my personal sphere has been hit by the virus. So relatively speaking, I am doing okay.

And yet...some things, some very significant things, seem to be being set aside, as if their importance is somehow diminished in reflection of current events.

My friend Sandie put this into words, and I don't think I can do any better.

"I can understand that Adrienne is feeling well enough now to have "all" the feelings of what has happened. Because she couldn't have the feelings when she was fighting for her life."

Adrienne, her Dad and I had a long video chat on Friday, the anniversary of the day the long path to remission actually started. The day the tumour came out. As part of that conversation there was a candid discussion about trust, about vulnerability, and how the only person that Adrienne felt she could be that vulnerable with was me. Not her Dad, not her sisters, and definitely not her friends. Just me. As a result of that, no one outside of that tiny, tiny circle of two has a true idea of what it was like for her. And while there were many upsides to that, there is one big downside that is slowly emerging.

Relatively speaking, her life appears to be okay.

News flash...it's not.

She is still dealing with social isolation when she desperately needs to get her life back. Right now is no different for her than it was for the last year, when she had to isolate herself from the world, from her family in Barrie, to protect not only herself but everyone else in the chemo clinic. But the difference is now that the physical battle is done, all of the emotions she successfully kept at bay for a year are rearing their ugly heads, making it difficult, sometimes literally, for her to breathe. There is a whole layer to how this is affecting her that no one understands. And she is stuck in a Groundhog Day scenario where she keeps waking up to the same reality, and there is nothing she can do to break out of it.

Is she lucky she can work from home? You bet she is, and she does not dispute that. She knows she's lucky to be working at all. She knows she's lucky that she was prepared practically to be locked into her house because she's been doing it for a year. She knows she's lucky that with me gone there are people in her life who will bring her food, bring her medication.

She knows she's lucky to be alive. How many of us genuinely, because our lives have been threatened, REALLY threatened, can say that?

My message to those around her is...

Expectations = must change.

Because relatively speaking, she is not okay. Just as going through the physical recovery from what she has been through will take a while, the emotional recovery will be a experience in and of itself. She has reached out, found an online group of young women like her than she can communicate with because they can relate to her situation. She is being honest with herself, allowing herself to feel the anger, to express it in safe places. But only a tiny bit at a time, because that's the only way she'll survive it.

She'll get there, eventually, but she is definitely not there yet. So, patience, sensitivity, understanding. Please.

You Couldn't Make This Shit Up Part Deux

Adrienne had an appointment at the hospital for her every three weeks Herceptin treatment today. Because she is trying to stay in her house as much as possible, she planned to kill all the birds with one stone today, so armed with her mask, gloves and disinfectant wipes, she set out on her way. She figured she could hit all the key locations, like groceries and the pharmacy, in about four hours max including treatment time.

The best laid plans of mice and men...

She got out to her car this morning and it was dead. Nothing. Thankfully her landlords are home due to social distancing so she was able to get a boost to get her on her way.

Then when she got to the hospital she had to line up because they have very serious screening systems in place to make sure that if you don't have a reason to be in the hospital you don't get in. They even give you a sticker...a sticker?...to say you passed. Like if you voted, or did well on your spelling test. "Congratulations...you are not a purveyor of pestilence and destruction. Can't guaranteed someone here isn't, though, so...enter if you dare."

As far as Adrienne was concerned, this was just going to be a Herceptin treatment day, but oh no. First off, bloodwork. Her inner arms are a mess with stress induced eczema, so first they tried one arm, then they tried the other arm, and then someone else was called over and they finally got it out of her hand. Can you say OUCH?

Then instead of just going in for her treatment, she finds out that she is supposed to see the doctor today. But not her doctor, not the one she has trusted with her life, but another one. But...because she didn't know about the bloodwork she had not allowed time for it, so by the time she got back to the clinic she found out that they had been looking for her but both the doctor meeting rooms were full so the nurse took her into the doctor's working office, where the doctors go in between seeing patients.

"So are you taking any pills yet?"

"Um, no...?"

"But your oncologist talked to you about using something for ovarian suppression, right?"

"Um, yes...?"

"Okay, good Here's a prescription for Tamoxifen. Any questions?"

"Um, no..?"

It was over and done just like that, and she felt like a stunned wonder, but because she was late she then was rushed into the treatment room.

BTW...

This medication actually has a LOT of side effects, it's something she'll have to be on long term, and she doesn't really know a lot about it, so does she have any questions?

OF COURSE SHE FUCKING DOES!!!

And now she has to wait for another three weeks until the next Herceptin treatment to ask them. Or Google it, which as we all know can be a simply terrifying proposition.

The matter of fact way that some things along this experience have been treated is truly mind boggling. Today was a perfect example, the feeling that you're being pulled along on a rope behind a horse and all you can do is hold on for dear life and hope in the end you're not too damaged to continue functioning.

Then, when she got out into the parking lot her car wouldn't start…again. She called CAA and the guy said yup, you need a new battery but I don't have the one you need on my truck. Another truck comes and the guy gets out and LIGHTS UP A CIGARETTE in a hospital parkade, the three foot no smoking sign two feet from his head. Adrienne looked at him and said the equivalent of…

"Dude…seriously?"

It doesn't end there.

She goes to pick up her prescription and the pharmacist looks at her pityingly and asks if she has had treatment. Adrienne list the treatments she's had and the pharmacist looks at her with THAT face and says…

"But you're so young."

That pharmacist has no idea how lucky she is that she is still alive.

You just couldn't make this shit up.

The Neverending Story

There's this common thought out there, in the Cancer Muggle community, that once surgery, chemotherapy and radiation are done that cancer treatment is over. While that may be the case for some cancers, it most certainly is not the case with triple positive breast cancer. Because this particular type of cancer feeds on hormones that are naturally produced by the female reproductive system, once the traditional treatments are over and for lucky ones like Adrienne the reproductive system kicks back in, there are a new set of longer-term life saving steps to stop her body from producing the hormones that could give the cancer a second shot at killing her. And research shows that those second shots tend to be a lot more successful.

Last week Adrienne started taking Tamoxifen. According to BreastCancer.org, here is a list of the side effects.

- o Hot flashes
- o Irregular periods
- o Vaginal discharge or bleeding
- o Mood swings
- o Depression
- o Weight gain
- o Blood clots
- o Endometrial cancer

Adrienne has to take Tamoxifen for five to ten years. The only break she'll get from it is when she decides she would like to try to have a child. She also may stop taking it during the five to ten years because she decides to have her ovaries out, which is the best treatment option to protect her from recurrence. That will throw her into instant menopause, but I am guessing it won't be any worse than the games Tamoxifen will play with her in the meantime.

This afternoon Adrienne sat outside alternately laughing and crying for an hour. In her words, like a crazy person. She chuckled about it when she told me, because it *is* crazy, and I can't quite reconcile that she has to potentially go through five to ten years of this.

Considering the current state of her life, the requirement for her to stay trapped in the same space she has been trapped in for over a year because of the cancer, she can't even be sure it's the Tamoxifen making her feel that little bit extra out of control today. Or if it's just one more rock piled on top of what is still her burden, the trauma that she is slowly but surely letting out of the box. The trauma that is a gift that keeps on giving.

She sent me a picture of a bunny in her back yard today, full of excitement that they are back. The bunnies appearing were special moments that lightened our spirits whenever we saw them, especially during The Awful. I think the universe, which has known all along the path that this diagnosis would take her on, sensed her tears today and knew she needed a little bit of a lift. And as you all know, her lifted spirits mean mine are lifted as well. Being this far away from her hasn't changed that. Maybe it's my turn to say...

ADRIENNE...YOU'RE A JUNIOR WITCH!!!

But a Nora Roberts Irish witches sort of witch. You know, the good kind. Not the kind that gets endometrial cancer after she already battled breast cancer. The kind that things all work out for in the end. That's a plot choice that I can get behind in this Neverending Story. Are you with me, universe?

Please say you're with me...

Memories...A Good One

The night before Adrienne's last day of chemotherapy, the atmosphere in the house was all over the place. It was a very significant ending, as you can imagine. When you've been going to the hospital for twenty weeks to have poison pumped into your veins and then spending most of your time dealing with the side effects afterwards it becomes a pretty important part of your routine. As a matter of fact, it becomes the center of your existence around which all other things are planned.

A friend of Adrienne's had picked up some low dose THC tea for her earlier in the process to help her with sleep. It was very helpful easing Adrienne down when her mind wouldn't stop racing, and she would use it to help herself relax enough that she could drift off. When she ran out of the tea the friend tried to find her some more but it was unavailable, so she picked her up some oil instead.

Adrienne had received some high CBD low THC oil to help with the nausea after meeting with the medical professionals at a cannabis clinic in May. It was a game changer. It gave her the ability to eat when things were at their worst, or at least made it less of a challenge. The oil had also had a calming effect, which when your life revolves around battling cancer is a nice side benefit. So when she was struggling to settle the night before that last treatment, she decided to take some of the oil that the friend had picked up as a replacement for the tea.

As we were getting ready to go to the hospital the next day, Adrienne was a bit off her game, and I could see by the look on her face that something was bothering her. I assumed it was about what the day was, but I checked in with her anyway just in case it was something more.

"To tell you the truth, Mom, I'm pretty sure I'm still high."

Adrienne does not like the feeling of a THC high. It was one of the reasons she chose the low dose CBD/THC oil when she went to the cannabis clinic. It was the reason she didn't use marijuana products more during her treatment. So this was an...interesting development.

We always packed a lunch or snacks when we would go for treatment because it was often around lunchtime and when you're stuck in a chair eating is a great way to pass the time. The oncology clinic was REALLY busy that day so instead of one of the chairs Adrienne was put into a private room with a gurney for her and a chair for me. A short time after she was all hooked up she looked at me and said...

"Do you think it's too early for lunch? I'm starving."

Oh yes, you weed smokers out there, you know where this is going.

Adrienne ate all of her lunch in about 3.2 seconds, and then asked me what else was in the bag. I told her if she wanted it she could have my sandwich and after almost no protest she said yes. And she ate it. All of it. And the fruit and veggies. About fifteen minutes later she asked me if I could go down to the pharmacy and buy her some chips...not the little bag but the big one. As I was getting organized to head down she asked me if I could also buy her some chocolate, some mmmmmm Rolos please, Mom.

When I came back to the room she ripped open the chip bag and dug in. I had picked up two packages of Rolos (I'm not stupid) and although she told me that was too much and she'd save one for later they also got eaten on the spot.

As it turns out, the THC oil she got from her friend, the one she had taken the night before, was TEN TIMES AS STRONG as the tea and oil she had used before and it was supposed to be diluted using some other oil before use. Unfortunately, Adrienne didn't get that memo. She had taken the same amount she did with the oil she used earlier in treatment to help with her appetite when the nausea was at its worst. And it certainly did the job with her appetite when it was still quite obviously in her system the next morning.

I didn't laugh out loud, but I really wanted to, as my "*I don't like the feeling of a THC high*" daughter ate her way through the biggest case of the munchies I think I have ever seen.

Memories...

Retail Therapy

When Adrienne was undergoing cancer treatment, in particular radiation which was five mornings a week, most of the time the weather was not the kind where you go out for a walk. If it had been snow on the ground and cold but no wind, we would have bundled up and gone out. But for the most part it was windy and wet and miserable and since neither of us is a Call of the Wild sort of gal we were stuck inside.

In the beginning, after surgery, we would go to a local mall to do mall walks. Circle the top floor, take the escalator down because the stairs were a bit much, circle the bottom floor, escalator up, rinse and repeat. The mental challenge was the stores...the shoe stores, the clothing stores, the cosmetics stores...and how they cast a spell on us as we were walking by.

*"Come...take a bite of the juicy red apple *cackle cackle cackle*"*

Retail therapy is definitely a thing. And if your funds are limited because you can't work retail therapy can be a definitely bad thing. But when your life is an all encompassing cancer journey, where your options are limited because of treatment and the side effects of treatment, it's one of those things that you CAN do, either at store or online, so it can be really hard to resist the witch's call. And in this case, it's a bad witch, not a good witch like me.

I was in Canada for six weeks in 2012 because I had gone up to be with my Mom after a bad fall and my H-4 visa was delayed in processing so I couldn't come back across the border. Most of my family couldn't be there because of big things happening in their own lives, which is why I went up even though I knew I wouldn't be able to go home for a long time. I would spend my days with her in the nursing home and go back to my small hotel room and tuck in for the night. It was a rough time. There were moments there when the staff didn't think she was going to make it. And then she surprised us all by climbing back up the ladder of life, so I didn't *need* to be there anymore. But I couldn't leave.

One of the things I started doing was stopping at a second hand store on the way back to the hotel. I would wander up and down the aisles, sometimes for a couple of hours, checking out clothes, shoes, knick knacks. It was a way to stop thinking about my situation, my loneliness, my aching heart. So when I very much *needed* to be in Ontario with Adrienne, and retail therapy was becoming an issue, I suggested we go to the second hand stores to wander about for a while.

It was absolutely fabulous.

Considering that we were trapped together in a one-bedroom apartment, one of the best things about going to second hand stores is that Adrienne and I are very different sizes, so our searches took us to different places in the store. We would go in together, but the next time we were actually together was in the fitting rooms.

We would arrive at the fitting rooms with six zillion things to try on. If you've ever shopped at a second hand store you know that's the only way you can actually find anything that will work, because a size tag on an item in no way actually tells you if it will work for you. We did make some purchases, in my case mostly things I could pull on during winter days to get myself out of my pajamas. There were some amazing price-tag-still-attached finds, too.

But one of the most fun things about it the whole experience was finding *those* items. You know, the ones covered in sequins, or feathers, or beads, or sequins and feathers AND beads. The ones with unrecognizable and who-thought-of-putting-these together prints. The how-would-this-even-work things where the staff have put in on a hanger and you can't even tell what it is. The ones you're positive were designed as a joke by a designer wondering exactly how outrageous a design would have to be for people not to buy it. We would pull them out, catch the other's eye across the aisles, and share our finds. And we would laugh.

The visits were a couple of hours of the day when we could bite the apple and not break the bank. Hours where we could go through miles of racks, moving hangers one by one to make sure we didn't miss the perfect shirt. When I couldn't wait to tell her that I didn't think we would see more plaid at a Lumberjack Convention. In a sense it was time out of time, and when your days are centered around fighting a deadly disease, having an outlet like that can make the world of difference. I know it did for me. Even if you think it's not for you, I highly recommend you give it a try.

Now where is that zebra print bedazzled feather boa I picked up? I want to kick my masked social distancing walk up a notch today.

Hey Mr. Pavlov...Nice to See You Again

I love chocolate. Dark chocolate, milk chocolate, chocolate cake, chocolate ice cream, chocolate sundaes, chocolate cookies. If I bought chocolate leading up to Christmas I had to leave it at work in my locker so I wouldn't eat my way though it at home. Yes, really.

When I was with Adrienne, during The Awful I would eat a bowl of M&M's and a bowl of Goldfish Crackers when I tucked into bed at night. It was obvious to me it was a stress management thing, and that got driven home one night when I bought some M&M's in Barrie and forgot to bring them back with me to Toronto and when it was bedtime I had a small panic attack...OMG I NEED ME SOME M&M's. I literally got dressed and drove to the store to buy some.

The last time I ate chocolate was the week before Adrienne's last chemo treatment. It was a weird sort of transition and has culminated in the idea of eating it making me gag a little bit. I just can't do it. My mind has created a clear emotional association between chocolate and Adrienne undergoing chemo.

Chocolate isn't the only thing. I also can't stand the thought of eating a grilled cheese sandwich, another one of my very favourite things in the world. It was my go-to lunch in Ontario. The thought of eating one now makes my stomach turn. Same with turkey bacon. I ate turkey bacon sandwiches a lot, too. Walked by the section it's in at the grocery store today and felt my gorge rise.

Steak is an absolute no-go. That one goes back to The Awful and Adrienne choking it down to keep up her iron so she wouldn't need a transfusion. And just when Luc perfected his BBQ steak technique..*sigh* Red meat in general is in the same territory, because we had to try to eat it more than we would have to keep her iron up.

One I hadn't really noticed until the last couple of weeks is pizza. It's one of the standard Friday night meals around here...has been for years. I had it once, when I first got back, but I could barely get it down. No pleasure in eating it at all. Bite, chew, swallow, ugh. I just found out this evening that it's the same for Adrienne. We didn't eat pizza as much as we ate flatbreads, but that's close enough to pizza according our minds, I guess.

There are a few things I would like to add to that list that might help me shrink my waist line a little bit. Like beer. I drank a lot of beer when I was with Adrienne and it's actually a bit embarrassing how many empties end up in the corner of the kitchen by the end of a week now that I'm back home. But beer was a thing I used to take the edge off, and I guess my body thinks that was a good thing, that maybe I still need to be taking that edge off until I get a chance to fully process.

But come on, universe, couldn't you have taken me to the other end of the continuum and make me now crave things like broccoli or kale? Brainwash me into thinking ice cream tastes like dirt (or kale...dirt and kale taste virtually the same to me)? Make me averse to sitting on my comfy couch that slowly but surely sucks me into its embrace regardless of my desire to get up and do some Step Aerobics?

I guess I'll have to settle for not having everyone in my life have to hide their chocolate if I'm in the vicinity.

Hey Mr Pavlov, nice to see you again.

Relativity Has Different Lenses...Samuel L. Jackson Style

I went for a walk today, and I saw a man I have seen multiple times on the path. It's obvious by his gait that there is an issue somewhere in his body that makes his walk just that little bit more difficult. He doesn't wear a mask as we've all been asked to do and my thought today was that maybe he thinks the universe has already thrown the worst at him, and I realized that I thought the same thing at the end of 2018 and I was very wrong.

And what that made me realize is that I am one tough motherfucker.

And that made me laugh.

There is something about being out there, in the fresh air, listening to my book as I walk like an Olympic speed walker (yeah I wiggle my hips and wave my arms and look ridiculous) that is letting me take baby steps towards my new life. I push my old body to its limits, walking up the hill, and I can feel when I hit the wall and then feel the second wind kick in. I walk in a bubble of my own making, daring anyone to get close enough to pierce it, because it is the isolation with nature that I need the most right now and can't have.

Something else I realized today, feeling grateful that my body is still functioning as well as it is, is that I'm starting to see the relativity of my experience when compared with others. That has been very difficult until now. I have been trapped in the bulls-eye in the center of my own emotional circle, struggling to maintain a relationship with myself, and it has very much blinded me to the plights of others, what they are dealing with every day, things the universe has thrown at them whether they were ready or not. That allows me to still feel very angry, very devastated by my child's suffering, very fragile in my own emotional recovery and at the same time allow for the fact that there are others who, relatively speaking, have suffered more than me, survived more than me, traveled a more difficult road than me.

Compassion is seeping back into my spirit, and it is a welcome visitor that has been absent for too long.

I need to acknowledge that it is still almost impossible for me not to filter anything I experience through the last year. Trauma is like that. Like grief, its impact ebbs and flows, and as a friend of mine recently told me there are a lifetime of firsts other than the obvious ones than bring it back in overwhelming waves. Those are the surprising ones you're not ready for, and it's hard to get anyone else to understand their significance because they are so personal. They don't need to make sense, and to those outside of your trauma they may not. They simply are what they are. But at least now I will have compassion in my toolbox to guide me through both my own and others' resurgent trauma and the emotions that come with it.

Adrienne still has such a long hill to climb, so many walls to hit, so many second winds to grasp as she keeps on moving forward. So many unseen and unknown triggers that will bounce her around like a rogue wave. So many small things that will pull her back to the trauma. But I have no doubt she'll get there.

Because like mother, like daughter.

That girl is one tough motherfucker.

Stubbing My Toe

I'm a big fan of medical based TV shows. Shows like Grey's Anatomy, Chicago Med, and New Amsterdam. Now that I'm back in the land of having cable, I've been able to catch up on all of these using the wonder of On Demand. And believe it or not they are giving me insights, scripted words that are helping me to understand a bit of what I have going on.

Tonight I'm sitting here watching one of them and an oncologist asked a group of young people what it felt like to be a cancer survivor. If you're thinking that maybe I should have turned it off right then, you're probably right. I have actually had to turn it off for the moment to put these thoughts onto paper...so to speak.

"I'm scared. Even though I'm in remission it feels like I'm just waiting for it to come back."

Man, am I old. I still have cable AND I think of what I am doing as putting words onto paper. I also remember what it's like to program a VCR using the 249 page booklet just so I could watch THAT episode of Friends, you know the one where Ross and Rachel finally get together? OOPS spoiler alert! However, despite my advanced age and old habits I DO have the newest cell phone version in my family. BOOYAH!!

That was the commercial break, brought to you by my rapier wit. Now back to my feelings.

I'm scared. I know she's in remission but I'm still so scared it will come back. She fought so hard, went through so much, came out on the other end with her eyebrows intact (twice). She's back at work, feeling pretty good about things considering. She's doing Zumba classes online three times a

week with her cousin Michael who lives across an
ocean. She's experimenting with food, getting ready to move
into her new house, her house with no memories of her Mom
sleeping in the living room. Getting away from the couch
where she put her bald head in my lap so I could stroke it,
trying to ease the distress, the pain. I can't tell you how I
wish I could unring the cancer bell, so I didn't have to be
scared, so I could celebrate unhesitatingly.

I know I must sound like a broken record when I talk about
this never being over. It's just that, well, it's the truest
statement there is once the bubble of innocence has been
broken. Cancer is so sneaky, you see. It's like the evil twin
in soap operas that always comes back to ruin your
relationship by framing you for murder because he wants to
marry the girl, or the one that holds you in a cabin in the
woods pretending to be you so she can take over the
company Daddy left you even though she is the oldest by
seventeen minutes and it should rightfully have been hers.

Part of my healing, I think, is for me to realize that I will
always be scared. It will be a part of me like my baby
toe. Something that is there but that I don't actually notice
all the time. Until I stub it, then it's right up there in my
face. Not literally. You're welcome for the visual of me
having my baby toe up in my face.

My reality is that once in a while, like tonight as I was sitting
here enjoying my On Demand-because-I-have-cable medical
show, it will be like stubbing my toe. It will be sharp
reminder that it's still there. That it is a permanent part of
my existence now. That the fear will sometimes take my
breath away, and then will ease with time.

That sounds a little like I'm offering my own spirit some
compassion. I'm glad I found it again.

Seriously, now I can't stop visualizing how ridiculous I'd look trying to get my baby toe up to my face. Dammit!

April 29th, 2019

I started writing this story in May of 2019. I had been with
Adrienne for her first surgery on March 27th and come home
on April 19th for what I thought would be six weeks before
chemo started on May 29th. Plans did change and I had to
go back earlier than planned because of the second surgery
on May 7th, but on April 29th, 2019 I wasn't there. That was
the day Adrienne met with the medical oncologist for the
first time, the day that she found out that this would be for
the rest of her life.

I was there on speaker phone, to hear the information, to be
hit with the semi truck about what was to come. But I wasn't
there to help her absorb it, to hold her in my arms after she
got home after the appointment with the realization that her
hopes that her treatment plan might not be that bad had just
been nuked.

After the first operation, when the doctor came out to tell me
how it went, he told me that she would be a pretty busy girl
for a while, and when I asked him what he meant he told me
chemo and radiation both were in her future. I asked him if
her chemo was going to be like the pills her Grandmaman
was taking at home, and he sadly shook his head no, that it
wouldn't be like that. I remember being shocked and
disheartened at his response, but I pushed it aside in the
following days as I took care of Adrienne's body as she
recovered from the surgery. So I *knew,* but at the same time
I didn't know. Or maybe didn't want to know and took
advantage of the active mothering I needed to do at the time
to not think about it.

Looking back, one of the things I was shocked about, the
rapid growth of her tumor from biopsy to surgery, was I
think maybe a game changer for her treatment team as
well. When the surgeon first told her it was cancer, he called

it a little bit of cancer, a lump they would just go in there and take out. That was a far cry from his attitude on surgery day. I know hindsight is 20/20, but Adrienne is pretty good at reading situations and I don't think she felt that things were sugar-coated for her when she was told the news the first time.

That's the mindset we both had when she was going to meet the oncologist on April 29th, 2019. That it wouldn't be that bad. But it was so much worse than bad. It was devastating.

And I wasn't there.

I had one hundred percent planned to be with her on April 29th, 2020. It was going to be one of those anniversaries that I knew she'd need me, and I hoped that I could somehow ease the trauma of the memory. I could cook her a nice dinner, and then she could put her head in my lap as we watched some nonsense on TV and I could rub her back the way I always did when she wasn't feeling her best. Our tight little circle of two would close again until it was safe for her to step outside.

When I relatively calmly dropped her at the airport in Los Angeles after our little holiday in February, I could let go with the knowledge that I would see her again soon. We would go our separate ways, process a little or a lot, then come together and talk about how we were doing. Then we could share things that seemed to be working to break down the invisible walls we both felt trapped behind. How as individuals we were taking the steps away from the horror towards a life that was about more than cancer.

That on April 29th I could hold her. And feel her breath slow into an easier rhythm. And do what I could to take away some of her distress as the memory washed over her.

Once again, in my mind's eye I am sitting cross-legged in a meadow plucking a flower...and I know that the last petal that will fall is that she needs me. Like she did yesterday.

And I'm fucking STUCK here. I hate Covid 19.

Please...

Ask the universe for what you need, they say, and what you need will come with time. So I did.

I need the ocean, I said, tears streaming as the grief slid saltily down my face. I'm stuck here...my daughter really needs me to be there this week and I'm stuck here. Please...

The ocean is a healing place for me. I can stare at it for hours, listen to it all night long as it soothes my soul, stand on the edge as the water rushes over my feet, eyes closed, just being. Covid 19 has stopped me from seeking solace until two days ago, when in a moment of the universe's generosity I found a very small place, all their rooms facing the water, old motel style so no common hallways. I felt comfortable that we could travel to it while maintaining the social distancing I feel required to do to protect my family as well as all the other humans we encounter. I analyzed all the angles and realized that since it had a full kitchen, we wouldn't have to encounter any more people than we would have done had we gone to a grocery store. I went from my home, to the car, to the check in desk, to the room. I was face to face with one person, and she handed me the gift of a small bottle of hand sanitizer when she handed back my credit card.

As you approach from the east you can sometimes get little glimpses of the water between the hills. The first one I had today I started to weep. After we got settled I sat there this afternoon, seeing it, hearing it, feeling its balm easing into my mind with a warmth that I can't quite explain. I cried a few times, More than a few times. But there was a healing present in these tears. I texted Adrienne about it and she told me that she was having a weird sympathetic cathartic cry for me. She knows, you see, how much I was counting on being able to come here as soon as I got back from Canada. Although I did my best to put on a brave face, she was there, right there, and she knows me too well not to be painfully aware of how hard it was for me to watch her hurt. We did have a day in Manhattan Beach when she was here in February, and I know she could see how it was for me to be there. She was so happy to know that I had plans to be back for a week at the end of March.

We all know what happened there.

It's almost as if I was meant to wait just a little bit longer, though. Not so that I would appreciate it more, but so that I would be far enough away from the stranglehold on my emotions that I would be able to let go a bit. It was important that what I experienced today would be received as it should be...openly, rawly, completely. That it wouldn't get lost in the shuffle somehow. Because it was magnificent.

There is a red tide on the Pacific coast this week. As a result, the ocean put on a bioluminscent show as I stood there tonight with my feet in the water...an ethereal blue light flashing in the darkness along the length of the waves as they crashed ashore.

I stood there, sobbing, this time with such gratitude. And then I closed my eyes and just listened.

Welcome back, the ocean whispered to me. I've been waiting for you.

The Circle of One

Adrienne and I had a LONG talk yesterday. It started out as a group video chat between four households then it dwindled down to just us two. Funny how that circle still closes sometimes.

A while back I wrote about us not being able to process what had happened while we were together, and that is proving prophetic. I was there to offer Adrienne all the support I could, but I wasn't the one with cancer, and while we would share some things along the road to recovery I knew that hers would be different than mine. Since my return to California I have started to take some significant steps towards healing my spirit. I realized during our conversation yesterday that I have had the benefit of distance, emotionally yes, but more importantly environmentally. I do not have to live up to anyone's expectations. I do not wake up in the same place, sit on the same couch, walk on the same streets, shop at the same stores as we did when she was in treatment. I do not have to look at those stairs except in a picture. I do not have to live with those reminders every day, like she does.

Imagine if you will a rope unraveling, a rope that has been so tightly wound that it was impossible to tear it asunder. But it is not unraveling because it is broken. Rather it is separating into its individual strands because how it is, how is has been, doesn't quite fit the task anymore. In order for me to move forward, I have to separate from her. Adrienne told me before I came home that I would have to be selfish for awhile, to figure out who I am now, and she is very right. I have known this was coming for me. But what I have never told Adrienne is that I knew that eventually my own processing would leave her alone in a circle of one.

Which is what she realized this weekend when I went to the ocean. Which is where she is now. And it's a very lonely place.

She told me yesterday she feels like she's living a life of someone else's creation. And that someone is the Adrienne that she was up until March 15th, 2019. That person no longer exists. It's like being a fly on the wall in your own life, like stepping into a skin that no longer fits. It's close, it has some of the same characteristics, but it's not quite...right.

Adrienne's life was not a smooth road before the cancer. She learned many coping mechanisms along the way and had gotten really good at self-soothing her way past the bumps. But this ain't a bump, folks. This is Everest. And no matter how much she has tried all the tools she used before have not been working.

She thinks that the social isolation we are all experiencing right now has made it worse. I've been pondering that since our conversation last night and I'm not sure that's true. Adrienne is very self-aware and very observant of human behaviour...it's what she studied, after all...and depending on circumstances when she is with other people she will often become the version of herself that she thinks they need at the time, the one that makes things easiest. Not all the time, but enough. Her life was pretty good, you see, so it wasn't hard to absorb things from others. What she is going through right now is making that more and more challenging to do, in particular because she's not quite sure who she is. Her encounters with the outside world are pinpoint selective to keep her safe, and as a result her social network is very small. Even though it's a good one, when she is with other people she will appear to be listening, then find herself screaming at the top of her lungs inside her head. And when the screaming gets too loud she does one of two things...she completely shuts down, or she reacts, sharply. It's becoming clear to her that doing either or both of those things has to stop. Having all the time she has to herself has her looking very hard at what she needs in order to do that, and I'm not sure she would have been able to ask herself that question had she been with people all the time, engaging in her before-the-cancer-Adrienne habit of analyzing a situation and acting accordingly depending on the company she was keeping.

The wonder of this is to start that change she is poking through the invisible wall, and she is finding that there are more hands on the other side than she thought she had. Hands that are ready to hold hers as she grieves. Mine was the only one she felt safe with before, because it was just...a lot. But she is acknowledging that her healing village has to grow, and for that to happen she needs to be honest about how she is feeling. And despite her fear of letting them see, when she does, the hands still hold.

Imagine if you will the rope weaving again, and now it is coming together with more than two strands. As strong as that rope was, it would never have been enough to support her letting go of the weight she has carried for over a year. What she needs the most now as she moves forward is the compassion of others. She needs the space in the expectations people have of her, the image they have, so that she can figure out what she wants to be as finds the pieces to complete her new puzzle. She needs the strength of that rope holding together, understanding that all of that only comes with time. And once again I am so grateful, this time that there are people there who are ready to be there for her, who have always been there, really. She just needed to be ready to reach out.

She wasn't ready when it was a circle of two. But from her circle of one...

Schrodinger's Cancer...Part Deux

So where did I leave off in The Neverending Story?

Oh yeah, Tamoxifen. But before I move forward here's a recap of what else is still going on.

Because Adrienne's breast cancer is Triple Positive, part of her treatment includes a year of Herceptin treatments once every three weeks to prevent recurrence. Her last treatment...the last time she will have to walk into the oncology clinic, sit in the chair, be hooked up to an IV... will be July 14th. Until that is done, I will also not be done writing about this experience. (I already have a flight booked to be there for that treatment, 14 day quarantine upon arrival good to go because we have a PLAN!) Triple Positive breast cancer includes the cancer having HER2 receptors and Herceptin works by attaching itself to them on the surface of the breast cancer cells and blocking them from receiving growth signals. By blocking the signals, Herceptin can slow or stop the growth of breast cancer. It is an example of immune targeted therapy and can also help fight breast cancer by alerting the immune system to destroy the cancer cells it attaches itself to.

In Adrienne's medical oncologist's opinion, Herceptin is a game changer that stopped him from sitting in his office too many times with women and their loved ones in tears because he had just told them that their cancer had come back. She hasn't seen him for the last few Herceptin treatments and she doesn't know why he hasn't been there...vacation, professional development, the pestilence. The appointments are three weeks apart so a couple of them is a LONG time. Since she had a lot of questions about Tamoxifen and other next steps she was told during treatment would have to happen, when she saw that he was there this week she asked his nurse if it would be possible to have a quick chat with him about who or what or when or where or...? Turns out he wasn't busy at the time she asked so she was able to go right in.

Now, this is the guy who got really animated and excited talking about saving seven percent more women by using the more sledgehammer approach drug for ovarian suppression. The comment that stopped my heart for a second. This is the guy who talked about the importance of everyone having the long term goal of curing her and so taking advantage of all of the resources at his disposal was numero uno in the game plan. On Tuesday, when Adrienne asked him about ovarian suppression going forward, she fully expected that he would want her to switch from Tamoxifen to the more side-effects-nightmare ovarian suppression drug he had been so excited about a few months earlier.

So when he said that since she was planning on having a child within the next few years, and since she was doing Herceptin, he was comfortable with her staying on the easier drug, she was like...

"Huh?"

When she told me what he had said, for the very first time I found myself mentally disagreeing with him. Weren't you the one that got excited about that seven percent, Doc? Why now, after throwing the most powerful tools in your arsenal at her, are you choosing the less aggressive route? Come on, Coach. We're on the one yard line in the game of her life. This isn't the time to put the bench warmers onto the field!

But then it occurred to me.

In his mind, she's already in the end zone. He really believes that he killed it. He's lifted the lid off the box and he knows the fate of the cat. It's dead.

I wouldn't say this doctor was arrogant, but then again we never questioned his treatment plan, never looked for a second opinion. Perhaps because of that choice we were never on the receiving end of what that might have resulted in. All I saw was a man who was determined to save my child's life. And by golly, he thinks he did. It's taken me a few days to even seriously look at that particular little gem. It's very sparkly and has a huge wow factor, but to be honest I'm not fully ready to accept that it's real. Not quite yet. Still too much residual...stuff. Please don't judge. I think it's a pretty big accomplishment that right now I'm even able to put my hands beneath my chin and goggle at it in such wonder. And as I'm staring at it for hours on end from this angle and that all I can say is...

"Huh..."

Schrodinger's Cancer Part Trois (WTF Universe Part Deux)

Adrienne is physically fine. That's the type of WHEW OKAY opening I always ask for when the phone rings and it's someone who normally doesn't call me because my first thought is never...

"Oh I bet they won the lottery and they're calling to tell me they're buying me a house!"

Adrienne has been moving forward with her emotional recovery on a slowly but surely trajectory. Back at work, new home, a few road trips to fill up her emotional wellness cup with some hugs from the little people. A little retail therapy thrown in there to spruce up the new place (but no curtains... that particular fact is making me doubt my genetic influence). She is tentatively reaching out from behind the invisible wall to touch the trust bubble floating around on the other side, the one that will allow her to believe that the universe is done messing with her for the moment so she can take a deep breath and maybe pull some of that trust to her heart and mind when she pulls her hand back in. Or better yet, take a step into the other side.

Let's take a walk in the woods with Snow White. The animals walk along with us encouraging our pleasure by lifting up flowers for us to sniff, the birds land on our outstretched arms and chirp sweetly in harmony with our humming sounds. We're feeling safe and thinking the world is a pretty wonderful place. Then a darkness comes over the woods and the tree roots start to trip us up, their branches reaching out to pluck at our hair and scratch our cheeks. And then a bear steps out from behind a bush and smacks us in the face with a cast iron frying pan.

That's my girl this week.

Someone very close to Adrienne has to undergo a biopsy to check out some nodules in her lungs. *They,* the same *they* that reassured Adrienne that her suspicious lump wasn't cancer, have said it's highly likely that it's something benign. As you can imagine, it's impossible for Adrienne to have any faith at all that *they* know what they're talking about. She wants, so badly, to think that they are right, wants to be able to genuinely reassure this person that everything will be okay. She knows from personal experience, however, how much it slammed her into the ground when she trusted their reassurances before her own diagnosis, and she is too fragile in her recovery to be unprepared a second time.

It's not that she has completely lost faith in the system. That same system did, after all, save her life. But her faith is no longer blind, no longer trusting that *they* know-know. They are in the same place as everyone else is until the results come in. Until they lift the lid off the box and look inside.

Adrienne can simply not live in that glorious place of denying the possibility that in the case of her friend that the cat is alive in there. It's still wwwaaayyy too close. To keep herself safe she has had to pull herself all the way back into the bullseye of her emotional circle, telling herself to breathe, setting an alarm to remind herself to eat. So all I can say once again is...

WTF universe

Always the Outlier

Being diagnosed with Triple Positive breast cancer at the age of 27 instantly made Adrienne an outlier among breast cancer patients. It was difficult to find peer support because there just aren't a lot of them out there. As part of her healing process from the trauma while locked in during the pandemic she began searching to see if she could find mirrors of herself in the online community. She did find a group that seemed promising and tentatively began to watch discussions and then participate in them, especially when there were mental health professionals invited to host online events.

As the weeks have passed, she has come to realize that once again, she is an outlier. There are members of the group who have been more recently diagnosed or are currently undergoing treatment, and there are women five years in who are living with metastatic breast cancer in their thirties. As of yet, though, there is no one like her; diagnosed with Triple Positive breast cancer and after a year of treatment in full remission.

She had a treatment plan, she followed it, and it worked. There were times when she didn't think she could do it, when she would lie on the couch wishing she could go to sleep and not wake up. Not in the suicidal type of way. Rather in the way of knowing that the only time she didn't feel the full impact of The Awful was when she was sleeping. She sometimes has to stop herself from thinking she got off easy, because she didn't. My own guilt that my child survived when others have lost theirs, or when the treatment didn't work the first time, just had me adding in my head...relatively speaking. Survivor's guilt is a big burden to carry, and although I watched my child live through a nightmare she lived, and I even have to justify my feelings to myself.

There is a wisdom in having someone in the room with you when health discussions like how chemotherapy is going to go are being held. I wasn't physically there, but I was on the phone and I took note of a lot of things that in hindsight Adrienne doesn't recall her oncologist saying because she was simply overwhelmed. I say this because I had an "oh my" moment this past weekend when Adrienne was telling me about her feelings of not finding a fit in the online group. Here is one thing that I heard the oncologist say that she doesn't remember.

"I know this sounds aggressive, and it is. We went through a few years there when there was a question about using such aggressive chemo on younger patients with early diagnoses to avoid the side effects, and the oncology field's choice to ease up meant that I would have patients sitting in my office eighteen months after leaving treatment with metastatic cancer because we didn't go after it hard enough the first time. I refuse to take that risk anymore."

Oh my. The women in the online group Adrienne found who have been living with metastatic breast cancer might be those women. They might be the women who thought they were getting off easier than those who had come before, unknowingly avoiding the loss of their eyebrows in exchange for recurrence. They might be the subjects of a well-intentioned scientific experiment trying something new only to find out it was a mistake. A life shortening mistake. These young women...someone's daughter, someone's sister, someone's everything...might have made my child an outlier and are partially responsible for her being in remission.

Because they're not.

I need a minute...

Rebels with a Cause

Adrienne had the third-to-last of the eighteen Herceptin treatments this past Tuesday. We were very lucky Adrienne was diagnosed when she was because I could be with her during treatments, which cannot happen now unless an interpreter is required. The hospital has tightened up quite a bit on who gets in and it's easy for things to get backed up if there's even a small glitch. That happened this week, and when the intake person was on hold to check out another patient, she asked Adrienne where she was going and when she said oncology they just waved her along. Funny how that happens.

"We're not going to keep you here as we pile up and social distancing gets compromised when you have no immune system".

Which Adrienne does now, but they don't know that.

During the chemo part of her treatment Adrienne and I developed relationships with a few of the nurses that went just that bit beyond...as in one of them wept with joy when Adrienne finished her last chemo bag which meant she had made it all the way through in one shot. Another one of the nurses is ten days older than Adrienne, so there was an instant connection there since she was fully aware of the difference in impact between someone like Adrienne and a seventy year old patient because she could relate it to her own life in the moment. That came into play on Tuesday when Adrienne was approached and asked...

"We have someone young like you who is really having a hard time. Would you be okay with talking to her?"

Adrienne told me her gut response was whatever she needs, and she went with that.

When Adrienne went around the corner the young woman was sitting there weeping, her bald head covered by a beanie, with no one there to wipe away the tears. The nurse was with her in the middle of slowly infusing the red chemo. Remember the one that burns your skin if it leaks out, so they have to do it slowly to make sure it gets where it's supposed to? Yeah that one. The one that was part of the duo we call The Awful.

And yet Adrienne didn't even pause. She moved forward, stood beside the chair and started talking to the young woman, asking questions and giving answers as she could. The tears slowly stopped, and when it was Adrienne's turn in the chair the young woman came over and sat with her chatting while the Herceptin went in. And they joked about things that only people who have or have had cancer are allowed to. Things like...

Turns out they are both middle children, and they agreed that as middle children they needed to do something big to get more attention, so they went for cancer.

Turns out if the young woman hears one more time how strong she is...Adrienne finished the sentence with *"You're gonna punch them in the throat?"*

Turns out neither of them ate enough kale, and they both drank too much wine (probably to wash down whatever kale they DID eat because kale tastes like dirt...in my humble opinion).

And the things that weren't funny. Like side effects. Like infertility. Like losing facial hair. Like having to live dependently again after a long period of independence. Like looking around you in the treatment room and realizing you are so alone.

In the end they exchanged numbers, Adrienne leaving it up to the other to reach out. It wasn't until Adrienne was driving home that it started to sink in that as she sat with this young woman, she had been looking in a mirror over her shoulder. This is where she was a year ago. Adrienne knows that there is still worse to come for her new friend because she's been there. She knows there are many more fingers to be broken, many more times wishing she could not wake up. She texted me a "*Can you talk?* as soon as she got home because she was in a pinball machine of emotion, the ball bouncing back and forth between edges and paddles, bells clanging and lights flashing as it did. She had been trying to take a breath but needed a little help to get there, and she knows that right now I'm the best person to guide her through those times.

As she wound herself down what became clear to my daughter is that while she has memories of The Awful, most of them are still buried under the weight of horror she's still processing. She's starting to be able to *see* the memories...see herself in the chair, see herself laying on the couch, see herself with no hair. But she can't quite *connect* with them, like what happened to her happened to someone else. And though healing her own wounds will not be the primary motivator, she thinks that it will help both her and this young woman if they stay in contact. They will be part of a new circle of two, able to share things with each other that no matter how I tried I couldn't quite fathom.

Not because I didn't try. But because I wasn't a "you're so young" woman with cancer.

I'm keeping my fingers crossed for them, but only time will tell if they become a couple of middle child rebels with a cause. I really hope they do.

The Body Remembers When

There's a tune by Trisha Yearwood I really like called "The Song Remembers When". It's about a song on the radio that takes the listener back to a specific place and time, tossing a lighted match into her soul. One of my favourite lines goes "And even if the whole world has forgotten, the song remembers when."

I think there are many different kinds of things that time travel us that way. The smell of your grandchild's head the first time you snuggle in. Lilacs growing on a pathway as you meander by. Seeing Star Wars and remembering where you were the first time, in my case at a drive-in theater in its INITIAL RUN.

Driving to the same hospital for a potential cancer medication side effect related appointment where a year ago to the day you went in for your first pretreatment blood work before The Awful began.

Adrienne didn't cry at all last year on that drive. I'm not sure what was going through her mind. I didn't ask. Whatever mental bubble she had constructed to get her through it deserved my total respect and protection, not my probing. There were also logistics to handle like figuring out where the lab was, getting a parking pass and putting together a grocery list for us to pick up on the way home. It wasn't, in the moment, that big a deal.

But this year she cried...almost all the way there.

This is the known versus the unknown. She didn't know when she sat in the chair for that blood draw just how fucking horrible things were going to get. She most certainly does now. And to repeat what my friend Sandie said Adrienne didn't have the time or energy to experience all the

234

emotions related to the treatments when she was in the trenches. She just had to put one foot in front of the other and let her fingers be repeatedly broken. But in the last few weeks she's been finding out just how much her body remembers when.

The anxiety that she had to shove into a corner last year in order to function will not be denied its day in the sun as the anniversaries come and go. She is dealing with all of the *"I don't want to be doing any of this"* feelings right now as if they were happening for the first time, because in a sense that's exactly what's going on. Without the need for the first wave physical battle to be her main focus, because that battle has been won, the second wave emotional attack is racing across the battlefield and it's a tough fight because the troops are still exhausted from the last one.

This week Adrienne has been visited by the ghostly presence of chemo related nausea. It's like The Awful has snuck into her body as an ethereal being, settling in for a second round of misery. It's not the kind that has her lounging around a toilet bowl. Fortunately for her with the combination of drugs and more drugs it never quite got there the first time. It's the kind that is always just there, hanging around in the background becoming sharper or blurred depending on how distracted she is by other things. And when you are having to isolate at home there aren't a lot of those.

To ease it a bit, she ate some watermelon, because her body remembers watermelon helping the first time.

I used to cut that watermelon in small pieces so she could just pop them into her mouth. Typing that has dropped a lighted match into my soul because my body remembers how I used to ache for her going through such suffering, and the tears I couldn't shed then are in this moment flowing down my face.

I need a minute...again

But hey, she looked FABULOUS!

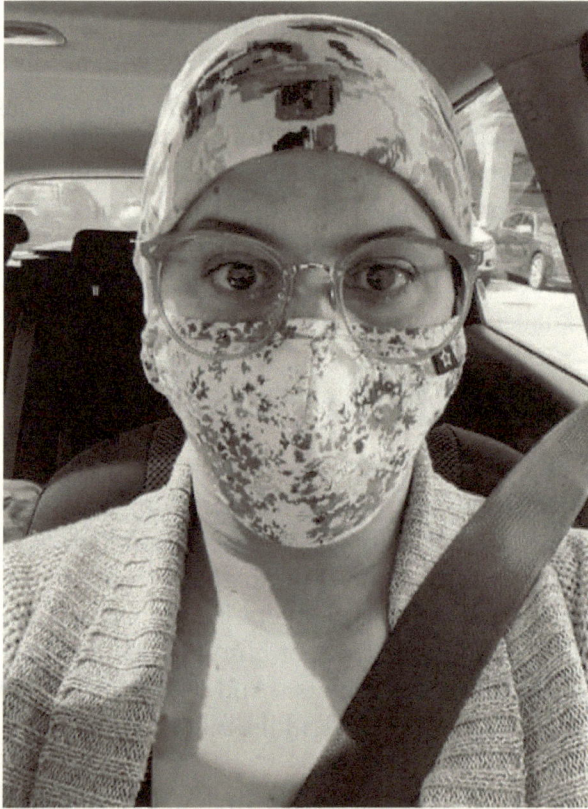

Making New Anniversaries

Me and my medical nighttime soap operas are at it again. I watched a show last week and a doctor had just found out that her son-in-law had cancer and she said to her colleague...

"We are now in the after. The after when you know about the cancer. When you know life is going to be hell, at least for a while. They are still in the before, making plans for dinner tomorrow, and now we have to go into that room and drag them into the after with us."

Sometimes writers just nail it.

My friend Sandie has been keeping up on my writing and after reading the most recent installment she sent me this...

"Hello. I just read The Body Remembers When. At the end it says, "I need a minute". What you and Adrienne need in my opinion is a year. You both need remembrances that are not The Awful. With such horrific times you need space, so you can say "Last June we (insert something joyful)", not a remembrance of things that happened because of the cancer. Once you both get to a new start you might feel that life is moving on and you're not just stuck with just anniversaries full of pain and suffering."

I've been thinking about how both of these thoughts, those of a script writer and those of my friend, tie together. There are two afters here. One was finding out she had cancer. The other was finding out that, at least for now, she doesn't.

There were huge emotions at play during the first after, when Adrienne was going through treatment after treatment, surgery after surgery. There were thoughts she had that she is only now sharing with me about how close she came to giving up. It was that bad. Remember when I had questions about who she did it for? Turns out that it was partially for me, for the others who love her, and I'll take that.

In the second after, the operative phrase is "at least for now". That's where the before and after part of that script writer's words hit the nail on the head. I think once you've had cancer, you can never *not* have cancer again, not really. It's part of that being prepared thing that keeps you sane. And Adrienne is not of an advanced age where the rest of her life is a relatively short period of time. She hasn't "lived a full life and it's sad but...". She isn't even thirty yet. She has a LONG time to live in the second after.

She has been talking to me openly about what she would do regarding treatment if it comes back. How her choices would be impacted by a lot of things, like who is depending on her.

"If I have a twelve-year-old daughter or son then I fight. If not..."

And there she shrugs.

I needed a minute with that one, believe me. I thought I had a handle on just how bad it was. Apparently not.

These big conversations are happening this weekend while we are making new memories...floating on a lake in perfect weather, sitting around a campfire, watching baby squirrels dart among the branches in the trees overhead. We haven't been alone together since we've been in a place where we have had time to individually reflect on our thoughts and experiences. We went to our respective corners and now we are sharing what we found there. We are having a just us weekend, and we both needed it so badly. She told me that many of these thoughts she can share only with me, because

I was there. I feel the same way. There have been oceans of tears and buckets of laughter, and the raw honesty has been such a gift. It's one thing to have a thought running around in your head. It's quite another to say it out loud, to see how it tastes as the words drift by your tongue. To think it was rotten somehow, then be surprised by the subtle sweetness it has when it's accepted and validated.

Sandie also said...

"I wish we could speed time forward and give you the distance you both need. Leaving The Awful on the side of the road, as you both speed forward in your new shiny car."

This weekend has given me a momentary glimpse of that. I think I actually sat in the car and admired the stylish interior.

And once again I am so grateful. The world is a crazy place right now, and I got to have a moment of peace with my daughter. We made a new anniversary.

Can't wait for next year.

She's Getting Her Hair Cut

Talk about coming full circle.

My girl is getting her hair cut. It has grown in enough that
she needs her stylist to do something to tame the crazy curls
that are framing her face. She's using fancy hairbands to
dress it up, and fifties era scarves when she wants it up and
out of the way, and it looks SO cute. Every time I have seen
her in the last little while I have had to resist just sitting there
running my fingers through her lustrous thick head of
hair. She might even let me do it if I asked, because she
fully acknowledges that I'm weird, but I feel like it might
push the envelope of humoring the Mom. I might ask next
time though, just so that I can replace the memories of
running my hands over her hairless head when it hurt so
badly she couldn't think.

She's getting her hair cut because she *wants* to. Not because
she *has* to. Wow, right? It's so incredibly exciting. I'm still
in the wow of it, I really am...annnndddddd here comes the
but. You knew it was coming. Let's face it...we're still on
the roller coaster for a bit.

When she told me that today, I was flooded...no, not
flooded. I was hit with a hurricane of all the emotions I had
not been able to fully feel when she sat in the chair to get her
hair cut off in preparation for losing it to chemo. It's the
same chair she'll be sitting in in two weeks from now to get
it styled so I can picture her there. It was like a weird movie
special effect where I was sucked back in time and zapped
from scene to scene; holding her as she cried the night
before, helping her in and out of the shampoo chair because
she was still recovering from surgery, watching her come out
with it shaved off. And all the tears I needed and wanted to
shed then but couldn't came pouring out of my eyes.

I sobbed. I sobbed out loud. I found it hard to catch my breath. It was ugly in all the beautifully ugly ways tears can be.

I always look for a good analogy and here's my take on this one. It's like I was Pinocchio and now I'm a real girl. Cancer was the puppeteer, moving my legs and arms willy nilly in a dance over which I had no control. I thought I had cut all of the strings, but every once in a while, something comes along and jerks me off my feet leaving me dangling helplessly in the air. It comes on with such shocking force. I had gotten so good at controlling my emotional reactions when feelings hit me like that for such a long while there and now, well, I suck at it. I try very hard every time not to be eaten by the whale but sometimes it just swallows me up and thankfully there are more and more joyful things in my life as each week passes that help me light the fire so I can get out.

This is my life now. This is my new norm. I'm not sad. I'm not depressed. I'm not even angry all the time anymore. I just need to be prepared for a rutabaga to send me off into paroxysms of uncontrolled sobbing. I'm thinking I'll get one of those smiling masks, just to confuse people in the grocery store when the vegetables set me off and I'm sobbing behind a piece of cloth featuring a cheeky grin.

I'm so dark and twisted. Now I have you wondering about the rutabaga.

Muahahahaha.

The Little Things...Part Quatre

This past weekend I got to go visit Adrienne. She had read my last entry and with a cheeky grin on her face asked me if I wanted to run my fingers through her hair. She shifted over and laid her head on my chest and I sat there for at least at hour just playing with it. It's so soft and healthy and shiny and curly. It's so strong. Of course, because it's hair by the time I was done she looked absolutely ridiculous. I so love her that she just let that be okay, that we laughed together about what my play had resulted in.

The hair thing reminded me of another factoid about cancer treatment that isn't in the public playbook. Yes, your hair falls out. But the reason your hair falls out is because the chemotherapy drugs attack the fast-producing hair follicle cells as they attack any cell in your body that does its job quickly. That's because cancer is fast. Once it gets on a roll it zooms into a reproductive process that would be the envy of any manufacturing wunderkind. And chemotherapy drugs, like your dog, can't tell the difference between the poor kid delivering your pizza or the axe murderer who just escaped from the mental institution so when either shows up at the door there's a frenzy of activity. And just like the bite of the dog would be very painful for either of those perceived intruders, the attack on the hair follicles HURTS.

That's why I rubbed her head so often. Because it hurt. We made a mixture of oils and she would sit on the couch with me on the back of it straddling her and I would gently run my fingers over her scalp trying to make it feel a little less sensitive. Sometimes I would have to use only the tips of my fingers because more than that would make it worse. When she would lay her head on my lap, I would carefully lay my hand on it trying to infuse some calming heat.

The brain is an amazing machine. If there's an event or a loss that's too traumatic it has a way of walling itself off so you can survive the trauma. And then here come the memories. They come back in fragments and little puzzle pieces that you have to put together. And when that happens that hurts...it's an actual body ache. Like what happened to me when she told me she was cutting her hair. There are just so many memories that are associated with her hair being gone that need to be allowed to surface. It's like her new growth is a shield for me protecting me from all that pain, and her choice to cut some of it away took down a piece of my wall.

This is the memory I tried to start overwriting this weekend. She didn't know this picture existed until now. The timestamp is July 10th, 2019. I only took a few, but they were ones I knew I would need for both of us to understand as time passed just how real it was. Just how hard it was for her. Just how far she has come.

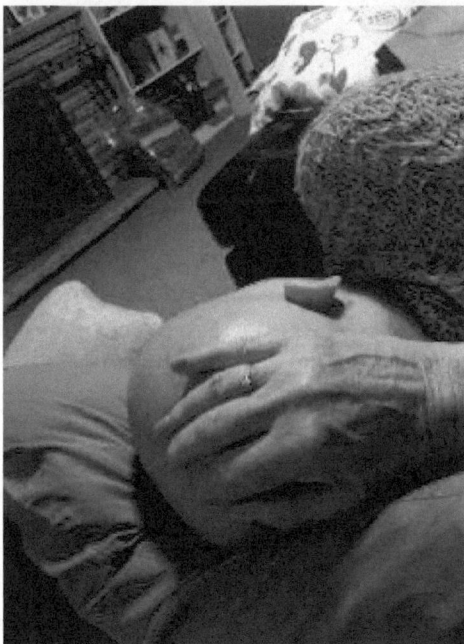

And this is a picture taken of her last week. Not even a year later. How can a body go through what hers went through, how can a young mind suffer so much trauma, and less than a year later look like this? There is such a maturity in this face. So much understanding. So much...more.

This weekend as part of my visit we did a fridge clearing party, at my suggestion. We found some interesting items but I'm happy to report that almost all of them were identifiable. I offered to do the dishes as she wiped down the fridge and one of them was a container lid with the letter "A" written on it in red sharpie marker. I stared at it in my hand for a moment and immediately started to weep. Adrienne heard me and turned around to see what was going on and took me in her arms and said...

"Oh Mom I know and I'm so sorry. I'm had many times to process what that letter A means and this is your first time."

That girl, that girl in the second picture, held me close as I experienced the memory of packing lunches for chemo days, with the letter A on her container because her sandwich was different. She told me that my recovery would be not be the same as hers as we sat in an airport lounge in February and she's not wrong. I got to walk away from all of the things that would bring back memories. I didn't have to shop in the same grocery store, drive down the same roads, wake up in the same space. But she did. And because of that she has gained so much strength since then, enough that she could lend me some to move past the moment. I'm not used to allowing myself to draw anything from her, but sometimes, because she has already walked a particular path, she reaches out her little hand in a giant gesture of comfort and understanding to me to pull me into safety.

I could not be more proud of her right now.

The little things...

Isabelle's Story

This one is going to be very difficult to write. I have walled off the emotions associated with it because it was impossible for me to look at them let alone feel them. I can guarantee that by the time I am done writing Isabelle's story I will have shed a few tears.

Isabelle is my youngest child. By the time we got to her I had pretty much figured out what worked and what didn't and what was really important...or so I thought. When I say that these three sisters have totally different personalities, I am not exaggerating one little bit. The best way to make this clear is to think of them as cups.

Stephanie was 3/4 full.

Adrienne was about half.

Isabelle's had a hole in the bottom.

Recently Isabelle has shared with me how much anxiety gripped her life as a child. When she wanted to sleep in her Grandmaman's room shortly after her Grandpapa died, I thought it was just concern about losing another grandparent. Turns out it was because Isabelle's room was closest to the front of the house and she thought if someone broke in they'd kill her first. In grade four she wanted to wear nothing but blue t-shirts, track pants and track jackets, so that's what I got her when I went back to school shopping. Turns out it was because deciding what to wear in the morning completely stressed her out. As part of her sharing she has acknowledged that how we handled a lot of these situations as a child helped her cope. Go figure. I just ran it all through the "Is it physically or morally threatening" filter and if the answer was no we went with it.

I have always been Isabelle's "person". Whenever something came up that she was having difficulty managing she would call me and I would do my best to help her process it. When she was living with Adrienne during the university years there were times I would warn Adrienne before she got home and she would stop at McDonald's for some nuggets and a grocery store for some Doritos to give as an emotional support offering as she came in the door.

Fast forward to 2019.

At first it was occasional vomiting. Just here and there when she was feeling a bit of distress. It didn't even have to be something big. A pizza date with her boyfriend resulted in her throwing up the pizza on the side of the road. They are still together, by the way. He's a bit of a keeper.

On March 15th, 2019, when I got the call from Adrienne that she had cancer, Stephanie had just a short time before that phone call messaged me that she had taken Isabelle to the hospital because she could not stop throwing up. She was sent home after some IV fluids and anti nausea medication and thankfully she had her sister's house to go back to. When Adrienne picked me up at the airport and we drove up to Stephanie's on Sunday, I walked into Stephanie's house to her telling me that Isabelle had to go back to the hospital because they had said if she got a temperature she needed to go back in. More IV fluids, more medication, back home.

A while later, I was with Adrienne when I got a message that Isabelle was back at Stephanie's, once again not able to keep anything down. Adrienne could not be alone, and as the day progressed she knew I was struggling big time. The situation not only impacted Isabelle, it also was putting extra pressure on Stephanie with her two kids in the house and an incapacitated sister in the basement. So compromise time. We would both go. The following morning, I had

Isabelle back at the hospital and after a 13 hour stay in emergency we were blessed with a doctor who figured out what was actually happening. Isabelle has Cyclic Vomiting Syndrome. New treatment plan, and it worked. And here's where Isabelle's story closes Book One and starts Book Two.

You see, she never asked me to come. She knew I was with her sister and she wouldn't ask me to choose. Isabelle needed me very much in that moment. I'm her person. I'm her Mom. I have always been a source of energy for her to tap into when she had nothing left. To make it worse, I wasn't a country away as I usually was...I could have been there in a little over an hour. But right then she understood that Adrienne needed me more. She knew in those moments that for the first time in her life, she had to do it without me. No warning, no time to get ready. Rug pulled.

Isabelle has gone through a lot in the last sixteen months, most of the events the sort of thing that would have put her on top of my kid pyramid. She knows that. I know that. She has pulled herself away from many things to allow her to create a stable foundation so that she can safely move forward. Funnily enough she has always done what she needed. I guess she just didn't realize that she had.

And we both know that in a sense life tossed her into shark-infested waters and I was too busy keeping someone else from drowning to be her lifeline. And while the obvious person that brings to mind is Adrienne, a lot of the time that person flailing in the water was me.

Oh my Isbabelle...you are so so loved.

Stephanie's Story

I can't even.

She has opened her home to all of us, not even blinking when her life was invaded without notice.

She has understood when plans had to change at the last minute because someone else's circumstances made that necessary.

She has forgiven forgetfulness.

She has accepted that her Mom is sometimes not as strong as she would like or need her to be.

She has been solid when everything around her was rocked by tremors of despair.

She has allowed us to absorb all that is good from her children when the joy they bring was desperately required.

She has been honest about her feelings when it was safe to be honest.

She has moved furniture from room to room to accommodate the ever-changing needs of her extended family.

She has been a realist in a time when reality was sometimes dark.

She has watched us eat chocolate when she can't.

She has allowed herself to be frustrated.

She has gone shopping on December 24th because Adrienne couldn't play the role she usually plays.

She has done her best to understand things that are difficult to understand.

She has gracefully allowed me to pass her the torch, passing it back to me when she sees that I would like to and am able to carry it.

She has married the perfect partner to allow her to be who we needed her to be.

She has been all I ever could have asked for when my life was turned upside down.

I simply can't even...

Don't Look Down

You know those commercials where you see a man in a suit ask someone what they'd do if they won the lottery?

Right now I'd need it to be a pretty big pot of money. An obscene amount of money. The kind that would let me buy seven islands just so I could have a new one to wear every day of the week. The kind that would let me save all the rain forests and feed all the hungry children. This of course is on top of me buying her a house, and her a house, and her a house, and her a house...

The kind that would let me buy a hospital and make them keep giving my daughter Herceptin.

Because today is the last time she'll get it. It's the last time she'll sit in the chair and have this game changing drug infused through her port. After today, nothing other than the luck of the draw and betting her life on the most recent science is going in to stop her cancer from coming back. Now we enter cancer purgatory...the five-year waiting game where nothing is in the arsenal other than the fact that it's supposed to be dead.

A friend of mine went through a year of punishing chemotherapy and when she went back for a follow up scan a while after it was done and it had a good outcome her response was pretty much...

"Okay".

People around her were over the moon about the result and couldn't understand why she wasn't all puppies rolling in the meadow and unicorns farting rainbows about it. But I understand. Oh boy, do I understand. Relief, yes. Taking the anxiety down a few notches, yes. Dancing naked in the rain? Not so much. Here's how it works.

If I think I have cancer, I go through the diagnostic tests and sit in a doctor's office with a fifty-fifty shot. Even odds that I do or don't have it. Even odds that it's some benign growth that won't do me any harm. Even odds that it's a cherry pit I swallowed when I was four that hid there for decades just waiting to cause alarm. That's the perch I get to sit on looking over the abyss, a spring-loaded affair ready to launch me over the edge that either gets triggered or doesn't.

Adrienne sat on that chair on March 15th, 2019 and that trigger got pulled, tossing her helplessly into a deep hole filled with pain and suffering that is only truly known in hindsight. She has scrabbled up the wall of the abyss inch by inch, many fingers being broken along the way, moving up only to fall back down and then push herself beyond her own limits to try again to reach the edge. It has been an exhausting process, both physically and emotionally, and today she will reach the top. But rather than climbing out, for now she will have to just hang there, off the edge, legs dangling, for a long time to come. For a sixth of her life. And it will continue to be exhausting.

I will do my best to shore up her efforts. I will step down from my perch and join my hands to hers when she needs to adjust herself to where she feels safer. I will encourage her, reminding her of how far she has come, assuring her that she has the strength to dig in and hold on tight. I'll remember when with her about the dumpster diving, about the toilet humour, about Clara wearing her wig so she'll see that there was always laughter. I will hold a mirror up to her sparkle so she can see how amazing she is, how in a world that turned so dark for her she never let that go.

And I will look deeply into her eyes and ask her not to look down.

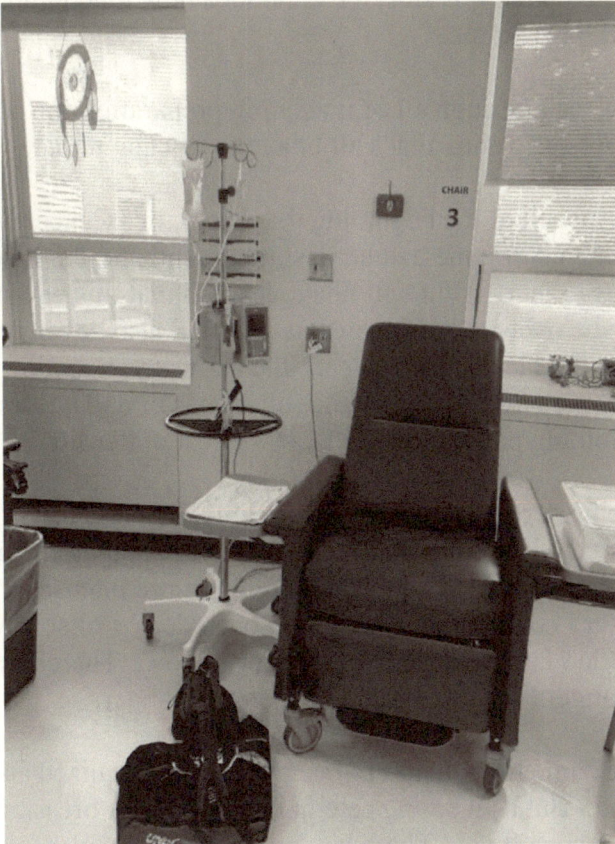

The End...

When I started this story I had no idea how much impact it would have on me.

I have read through all of it again in preparation for writing this last entry and...that's all I have to say about that.

I told myself at the beginning that Mom...It's Cancer would end when Adrienne had her last treatment, and I'm holding myself to that. Although I have learned that this will never really be over for Adrienne and so it will also never be over for me the fact is that this part, the active treatment part, is done. We have gotten off the roller coaster and we are now in a holding pattern that will last the rest of her life.

There have been more and at the same time less tears that I expected. There has definitely been more laughter than I thought possible. There has been fear more intense than I thought I could bear. There have been depths of sorrow that I couldn't fathom even existed prior to now. There has been such anger. Oh my, there has been such anger.

At the same time there has been hope, both realized and dashed. But as it springs eternal in the human breast, it has always been there. There has been joyfulness, playfulness, wonder. There have been reflections and realizations. There has been a connection created with my child that still amazes me a little bit in its other worldliness.

There has been a lot of beer, and a lot of chocolate. And a LOT of retail therapy.

But the one that stands out the most is this feeling of gratitude. Don't get me wrong here. I will never be one of those people who is so grateful that I wouldn't change anything. If I had the Infinity Gauntlet I would snap my fingers and make all of this disappear. In a heartbeat. I would never choose to have my child go through what she has gone through. I would go back in time to that office on March 15th, 2019 and have her doctor say that it was something, anything, benign. I would pick up the phone and hear her relieved voice telling me it was all good.

I would go back to the before.

But since I am stuck in the after in this neverending story, I will always be grateful for all of the gifts I have been given during this process. For all I have learned. For all I have been forced to accept and roll with. For all the rawness, learning exactly how much a person can survive. For all the sacrifices made. For all the people who were in my corner. For all the love that came my way.

For the fact that she lived.

The End...

Made in United States
Troutdale, OR
12/16/2023